CONTENTS

GREENFOODS
For Rabbits & Cavies

By F R Bell FRHS

Ninth Edition
(2007)

Revised and with additional chapters by Allan Trigg

ISBN 978 90 377 5115 4

Published by *Fur & Feather*
for
Coney Publications
Chattisham, Ipswich, Suffolk IP8 3QE

PREFACE

Although convenience foods may be the "in" thing in modern society and it is, admittedly, very accommodating for the busy and lazy person alike to feed one's stock out of a paper sack, there is not the same sense of pleasure, job satisfaction, call it what you like, compared with a more varied and natural way of feeding.

Also, I am sure that the more varied a diet you can give your stock, the better will be that animal's quality of life.

Of course, I do appreciate the pressures and changes in modern day living and very few people these days can pop over to the field next door and cut or collect a sackful of natural herbage. Hopefully, though some effort can be made to provide one's stock with as varied a diet as possible from cultivated green-stuff if not wild food and if I can give a little bit of a twist to a well known saying - A little of everything that you fancy does you good! I, myself, would not like muesli for breakfast, dinner and tea and so I apply the same thinking to my stock and give them as enjoyable and as varied a diet as I possibly can.

Living in town these days, means that I am reliant to a great deal on my allotment and the local market and the cultivated section of this book will be a great help to first time and established gardeners alike. In fact, even non-gardeners are likely to benefit and learn something. Likewise, with wild green food, I am grateful for F.R. Bell's literary guidance in the following pages and I have always tried to give my stock a mixed bag of green food so that they receive a balance diet with grass and astringent plants counteracting the laxative properties of others. In fact, even non-gardeners are likely to learn something and my only observation would be that perhaps some of his spacing between rows and plants is on the generous side for today's gardens An example of his "generosity" concerns beetroot where he leaves 9" between plants. 6" would be adequate. With carrots, he states nine to ten inches between each root but unless you are growing for show that's excessive. I would suggest 2-3 inches (6-8cm).

If the reader takes heed of the advice given in Chapter 1 – Principles of Feeding, the reader should not encounter any feeding problems or digestive disorders but it should always be kept in mind that *any change in diet should be introduced gradually*. Also, in today's world, increased traffic levels create problems of pollution that make roadside collection ill-advised in many cases. Elsewhere, dog, cat and even fox fouling is another hazard to be considered; especially in warm, wet conditions.

Whilst this little book should prove to be an invaluable help and reference guide, it should not be considered complete and exhaustive. If more information is needed, you could ask your local fancier friends or check the library for reference books. If these efforts fail and you still have a problem then I would suggest that you write to *Fur & Feather* and ask the experts.

Finally, I would reiterate the comments made by a former Editor of *Fur & Feather* as I hope the following will prove to be useful information :-

"They will find too, innumerable garden flowers and plants which the rabbit keeper need never let go to waste. They will not provide such enormous quantities of green food as are to be gathered from the hedgerows and countryside, but they will help. The small stock breeder can feed wallflowers, stocks, nasturtiums, forget-me-nots, double daisies, marigolds, borage, honesty, michaelmas daisies, galega, all prunings from rose, apple pear and hazel trees and the leaves and stems of hollyhocks, geraniums, heleniums and golden rod."

I have fed a few of these items myself although I would be reluctant to try rose prunings as the thorns can be vicious and I would have thought rather a dangerous proposition.

Allan Trigg

PRINCIPLES OF FEEDING 1

Many people and even experienced fanciers still persist that a domestic rabbit by its own natural instinct will not eat anything of a dangerous character. The writer maintains it is never safe to trust to the instinct of domestic rabbits in this direction, for although animals which are thoroughly healthy and well fed usually avoid deleterious plants, if a choice is available, a proportion of them will fail to do so, especially in the spring after months of deprivation, and it is, therefore, important that the owner should avoid putting anything into the hutches which is at all of a doubtful character.

Forewarned is forearmed, and speaking from my own personal experience and observation, I consider it is most important to give every thought as to whether green food is good, bad, or indifferent.

It is for this reason that I have written a book of this nature in order to help my readers to differentiate between useful green foods and those to be avoided. To keep a rabbit in good health and condition a large proportion of its diet should be a natural one. You can, therefore, see at a glance how important it is to have a thorough understanding in this direction if success is to crown your efforts.

Many people, including even those who keep rabbits on a large scale, have little knowledge of the various properties contained in the green food given to their stock, and although, so far as my own knowledge goes, no general analysis has been taken of all the plants and herbs that grow in this land of ours, yet a great many of them have recognised medicinal properties.

Speaking generally, very few green-stuffs are injurious if given in moderate quantities when well mixed with other plants, but a great number are endowed with medicinal properties, which manifest themselves by causing indisposition and even serious illness if such quantities of the plant are eaten as will constitute a 'dose' of the active principle some of these particular plants contain. It is, therefore, wrong both in theory and practice, to go out and gather a basketful of one particular sort of plant for your rabbits. No bad results will follow if each animal receives a small portion in addition to hay and other food; but if the gatherer had brought home a variety of food, each animal could have received a far larger proportion without any bad results, and it would have taken the place, and saved the use of, some of the other foods, such as hay and corn.

Another subject that often arises when discussing Green Food is the question of giving it to stock when it is in a wet condition. It is probable that the evil reputation earned by wet green-stuff is mainly due to the fact that it is easier to convey the germs of parasites to the hutches when it is in this condition. The writer has failed to find that even in the wettest weather it causes the slightly intestinal disarrangement if sound and clean and off clean land, provided always that your stock is constitutionally sound and care is taken to give a mixture of plants.

The main trouble today *(most probably due to indiscriminate inbreeding)* is that a great many rabbits are suffering from intestinal weakness, the result being that the least change of diet seems to upset them, and very often serious loss is experienced, as such stock so easily become scoured. The writer at this point does not wish even to suggest that inbreeding should not be practised, but that when inbreeding, every care should be taken to note there is not the slightest taint of any weakness on either side of the parent stock. At times inbreeding is necessary to fix certain points in the breed, but when the least carelessness is allowed, weak points are sure to manifest themselves in no uncertain manner.

Grass and green-stuff gathered for rabbits should always be chosen from open, sunny situations. Coarse long lush grass that grows in the shade, or in a damp situation, should never be given, as it is this type which will often be the cause of an outbreak of parasitical disease. Great care should also be given in avoiding all such plants that are mildewed or in any way diseased; and when gathering green food it is as well to notice that no fungus growth is attached.

These may appear small details, but they are apt to be overlooked by the gatherer in his haste to collect a bagful of green-stuff in double quick time.

Green-stuff is also very unwholesome if it has been allowed to heat, and for this reason it should never be kept in heaps, but should be laid out loosely on a clean floor, and those who will care to take the trouble will be well advised to place it loosely on wire-netting racks. By so doing they will be amply repaid for their pains.

Another mistaken policy is to glut a rabbit with an abundance of one particular green food. I always strongly maintain that there is nothing like feeding your stock with a variety of green food. Variety is the spice of life, and this applies just as much to the feeding of livestock as it does in any other walk of life. There is such a variety obtainable of both garden vegetation and wild greens that no fancier should ever be unable to give a mixed diet to his stock, and those who do so will always find their stock in hard, firm flesh and good condition of coat. Feed your rabbits on the same principle as you look after your own personal comfort. In our own daily diet we like a change, and this applies just as much to dumb creatures as it does to human beings.

Frosted greens or root crops also must not be given to rabbits however robust the latter may be. Any food so affected should be thawed and then used up quickly, as once they have been touched by frost they will not keep long afterwards, especially after they have been thawed. In very severe weather it is always advisable to keep such roots as are required in a warm temperature, and if at feeding time ten degrees or more of frost prevails, small pieces, which will be eaten up in a few minutes, are the most that should be given at a time. When a lot of trouble has been taken to thaw roots, serious illness will often follow because the owners have given more than the rabbits can eat up at once. The fragments left over have again become frozen in the hutches and the rabbits have eaten them in this state later on. As there is nothing more deadly than frozen roots, too much care cannot be exercised in this direction. It is obvious that whenever possible all roots should be stored where they are safe from frost, or be so well covered with straw that they are completely protected.

In the following chapters I shall advise you as to what are the most suitable crops to grow under cultivation should you be fortunate enough to have a garden or allotment.

And failing this, you need be at no loss regarding green food, as all the most suitable wild plants that are free for gathering will be described, and in many cases illustrated, and any outstanding properties these wild plants may contain will also be fully dealt with.

CULTIVATED GREENS & ROOT CROPS 2

Although it does not fall to the lot of every rabbit or cavy keeper to possess a garden or an allotment, a great many are able to enjoy this privilege, and for the benefit of those who have land at their disposal, I have decided to devote a portion of this book to the best and most useful crops to grow under cultivation, upon which to feed your stock throughout the year, and for the convenience of my readers I think it will be the best to deal with them in alphabetical order:-

ARTICHOKES, JERUSALEM VARIETY (*Helianthus tuberosus*) – The Jerusalem artichoke is a member of the sunflower tribe. It is quite hardy and productive of wholesome roots, or tubers, as they are called, and, apart from being a useful food for rabbits, they are in favour among epicures as a delicacy. By others they are regarded as worthless. It is said that wise men learn to eat every good thing the earth produces, and this root is a good thing when properly served; but when cooked in the same way as a potato it certainly is a poor vegetable indeed. It is a matter of some interest, however, that in respect of nutritive value it is about equal to the potato. Therefore, when growing it for domestic use we lose nothing in the way of food, though we are bound to cook it differently. Although it is useful vegetable for kitchen use it is not under that heading I wish to deal with it. Jerusalem artichokes are particularly valuable to the rabbit fancier for the following reasons:-

1. They do well in poor, heavy soils, which will not grow other roots or potatoes, and they can be grown again and again on the same plot of ground. The best results are obtained when the tubers or 'sets' are put into the ground from the middle of March to the beginning of April.
2. Artichokes have a very good feeding value.
3. They are particularly liked by rabbits.
4. They yield a heavy crop.
5. They are, comparatively speaking, frostproof, and can remain in the ground to be dug up as required during the winter. This peculiarity is one of importance to those who are short of storage room for such bulky things as roots.

Artichokes contain fourteen to fifteen per cent of sugar, two to three per cent of albuminoids, and about seventy-six per cent of water, and it is advisable that they should have hay fed with them. The tops *(leaves)* can also be used as food either fresh or dried, but mature stalks should not be given too freely, as rabbits are apt to eat too gluttonously of the hard and indigestible material.

Stock always enjoy the green leaves and you need never be afraid of scours when using them as food. On the other hand, they act as a deterrent to this complaint. Artichokes are grown from sets or tubers *(much the same as potatoes)* planted in the early spring, and can be planted in odd corners of the garden, where their height will not interfere with the growth of other crops. They are best planted in rows about 61-92cm *(2'-3')* apart, placing the sets about 30cm *(12")* apart in the rows and about 15cm *(6")* deep.

When the tops have appeared well above the ground, draw a little earth to the stems, in much the same way as you bank potatoes, and then leave the rest to nature. The tops grow to a great height, very often to 275-300cm *(9-10')*. The tubers can be used from the end of October onwards, so long as your crop lasts. I need hardly remind you to wash off the earth from them before using as a food for your stock. Artichokes are always appreciated as a change of diet once or twice a week when you are feeding extensively with other roots, such as swedes etc., during the winter months when greens are scarce or unobtainable.

BEETROOT, GARDEN BEET (*Beta vulgaris*) – As a food plant the beet scarcely obtains the attention it deserves. There is no lack of appreciation of its beauty for purposes of garnishing, or of its flavour as a component of a salad, but other uses to which it is amenable for the comfort and sustenance of both man and beast are often neglected. I have noticed how eagerly rabbits will eat beetroot when they have been 'off their feed', so to speak, regarding other roots.

The best kind to grow is the globe, or round variety as these can be grown with success on almost any kind of land, even when it has been difficult to grow the long beets successfully. To prevent them running to seed do not sow your seed too early in the year. The middle of May is quite early enough. Scatter the seed very thinly in rows, 30-38cm *(12-15")* apart, and when large enough to thin out do so to about 23cm *(9")* apart in the rows. The seed should be placed about 2.5cm *(1")* deep in the ground. The plants you thin out can be used as food.

A beet crop may be left in the ground during the winter if aided by a covering of litter during severe frost, but when the crop has fully grown to maturity it is better out of the ground than in it, and the proper time to lift it is when a touch of autumn frost has been experienced.

Dry earth or sand, in sufficient quantity, should be ready for the storing, and a clamp in a sheltered corner of the garden will answer if shed room is scarce. In any case, a cool and dry spot is required, for damp will beget mildew, and warmth will cause growth. In cutting off the tops before storing take care not to cut too near the crown, or injurious bleeding will follow; neither should you cut off the roots. A little experience will soon teach anyone that beets must be handled with care, as the goodness will run out of them. When using beets as food for your stock it is always advisable to feed liberally with hay at the same time.

Apart from being a useful crop to grow for your rabbits' food, beets are much appreciated as food for human consumption. When boiled from half an hour to two hours, according to size, allow to cool, then pare off the skin, slice, and serve with vinegar, and use in place of (or in) a salad with cold meat.

BRUSSELS SPROUTS – This is another very useful vegetable to grow, as apart from supplying the kitchen with a much appreciated addition to its menu, it will also supply you with a quantity of very nutritious green food for your stock.

The seed should be sown thinly in rows, in a seed bed that is situated on a warm, sunny border, in the early spring, say at the end of April or the beginning of May. Contrive to have the plants ready for pricking out by the time your early potatoes are ready for banking. Then transplant the more robust specimens 61cm *(2')* apart, between every other potato row.

These will continue to grow until such time as you take up your early potatoes, and they will then have become well rooted and firmly established, with the result that when you have taken up your early potatoes you will have left a good bed of brussels sprouts following on as a succession crop. As soon as they begin to grow into robust plants and the sprouts have begun to form you can begin to take off the stalk leaves and use them as green food for your rabbits. After the sprouts become matured, and you have gathered these for kitchen use, you can leave the stalks surmounted by the green tops in the ground to be used later on as a further and later supply of rabbit food. The stalks can be split into four parts with a knife, and they give your rabbits or cavies something to occupy their time when nibbling at them, as well as supplying them with a useful and nutritious food. Rabbits much appreciate a change in diet of this kind to nibble at.

CHICORY (*Cichorium intybus*) – I now come to one of the fancier's real favourites. This green plant should find a home in every fancier's garden, and as a cultivated green food it has no superior. It is easy to grow in any kind of soil, requires little or no cultivation, and is an exceptionally heavy cropper, as the plants supply several cuttings during the late spring and onwards until the end of autumn. Chicory is best treated as a biennial, and I shall deal with it on these lines. The writer has successfully grown chicory for a number of years with very good results.

In the first place, dig over your land deeply with the spade about a month before you sow your seed, leaving the land in a rough condition. If you have a supply of burnt ash available scatter it over the land. Failing this, use slaked lime in the same manner, and leave thus until the time for sowing arrives.

About the middle of June rake your land over and work it into a fairly fine surface. Then sow the seed thinly in drills about 1cm *(1/2")* deep, making the rows about 38cm *(15")* apart. At this time of the year you will find the seed soon germinates, and if the weather is suitable the first cutting will be ready in about six to eight weeks from the time you sow the seed. Successive cuttings will be available every two weeks through the summer until the end of October. After that time you will find rapid growth ceases. When you make a last cutting leave about 5cm *(2")* of green on the crowns, and you will find the roots will stand without harm in the ground all during the winter. When spring comes round the green will soon begin to shoot up again, and you will have a further abundance supply of green-stuff available until your new sowing is ready again. When the latter is ready, dig up the old roots of the previous year's sowing to make way for some other crop.

Although some people prick out separate plants into rows, I never consider anything is gained by so doing. It is far better to sow the seed very thinly in rows and leave it to grow undisturbed until ready for cutting. If, however, you notice bare patches in the rows owing to any of the seed failing to germinate, you can fill up these spaces by taking out a few plants from other parts in the rows where they have come up rather quickly. 28g *(1oz)* of good seed will sow, roughly speaking, about ten to twelve rows, each 90cm *(3')* long – that is, if you sow the seed very thinly. Some people will sow the seed more thickly and put 28g *(1oz)* of seed into six rows, each 550cm *(18')* long, or that equivalent.

Chicory is much appreciated by rabbits, and apart from being a very safe and useful green food to use it is also a splendid conditioner, and those fanciers who find pleasure in exhibiting will find it an ideal green food for producing that extra bloom on the coat that very often is the deciding factor in the awarding of the red card.

Brussels Witloof is the best variety of chicory to grow for use as a green food. It is obtainable from all good seedsmen at a reasonable price.

CAULIFLOWER – Here we have another double-purpose vegetable. The heart, or 'flower', serves the kitchen with a food most of us enjoy, and the leaves and stalks are regarded by all fanciers as a much-sought-after green food for their stock. Two kinds of this very useful vegetable are available, one for use in the late summer or early autumn, the other for use in the early spring.

The seed of the former should be sown in shallow drills on a warm, sunny border about the end of April or the beginning of May. When the young plants are large enough to be removed from the seed bed they should immediately be planted out in their permanent quarters. Although many people use the space between early potato rows in which to plant out their cauliflowers, the writer does not recommend this practice, especially if you have plenty of other land at your disposal.

The best results come from planting out on clean land that has been previously manured.

Allow the plants to be 61cm *(24")* apart in the rows, leaving a distance of 76cm *(30")* between each row. The early varieties so treated will be ready for cutting before the summer is ended. The kitchen will have the benefit of a useful vegetable, and the rabbits will be able to enjoy the outer leaves. The later varieties will be ready for cutting in the late autumn just previous to the frosts coming along, and furnish kitchen and rabbitry with additional food. Spring cauliflowers can be treated as regards sowing and planting in much the same manner as the other varieties, except that you sow the seed later in the year. The exact time for sowing is entirely a question of climate. In Cornwall and Devon, a good plant is secured by sowing during the late part of September or at the beginning of October, while north of the Trent many gardeners find the first week in August none too early. The soil need not be so rich as for your summer and autumn varieties, but still too poor a soil will not do justice to them.

When your young plants are ready for removal from the seed bed plant them out into their permanent quarters, and they will stand without harm throughout the winter. Immediately the warm spring days come along they will begin to grow apace. Spring cauliflowers are always in favour with the fancier as they grow such an abundance of outer leaves, especially at a time of the year when other greens are by no means easily obtainable. They also make a welcome change in your rabbit's diet and are much appreciated after a long spell of root feeding. I need hardly remind you how welcome a spring cauliflower for use in the kitchen.

When ordering your seed make it quite clear which varieties you require, whether for summer, autumn, or spring use, and then sow and cultivate upon the lines I have laid down. Cauliflower leaves and stalks are a safe and nutritious green food and can be given with every confidence to stock of all ages.

CARROTS – Owing to their richness in sugar and oil, carrots are liked by all stock, and have a reputation for being wholesome and easily digested. In consequence of their use for human consumption they usually fetch two or three times the price of swedes, and it is well recognised among stock feeders that their feeding value does not warrant their use at a much higher price than that which is paid for other crops. If, however, the fancier has a garden of his own he is in a much better position than the one who has all his roots to buy, and I always consider it a good proposition, provided the soil is suitable, to reserve at least a small portion of your garden upon which to grow this particular root crop. The carrot is a somewhat fastidious root for, although it is grown in almost every garden, it is not everywhere produced in the best style possible. The handsome roots of the *Long Surrey** that are seen in the leading markets are the growth of deep, sandy soils that have been well tilled. On heavy, lumpy land long, clean roots cannot be secured by any kind of tillage. Still, for these unsuitable soils we have the *Champion Horn** and intermediate varieties, which require no great depth of earth, while for deep loams the New Red Intermediate, *Long Surrey**, and the *Altrincham** varieties come in admirably. Before you choose which variety you intend to grow, a little careful consideration must be given as to what kind of soil your land is composed of, and then choose which variety is most suited to it.

For the main crops double digging should be practised, and if the soil is poor a dressing of half-rotten manure may be put in with the bottom spit. But a general manuring, as for a surface rooting crop, is not to be thought of, the sure effect being to cause the roots to fork and fang. It is sound practise to select for carrots a deep soil that was manured the year before, and to prepare this by double digging in the autumn or winter, so as to have the ground well pulverised by the time the seed is sown in the following spring.

The best time for sowing *(always provided the weather is suitable)* your main crop is about the end of April. Sow the seed in shallow drills, the distance between the rows to be about 30cm (12"). Cover the seed with a sprinkling of fine earth and finish the bed neatly. As soon as possible thin and weed the crop, but do not thin to the full distance in the first instance. This can be done gradually, as each time you thin out you have at your disposal a number of delicate young roots upon which to feed your stock. At the final thinning leave a distance of about nine or ten inches between each root.

The carrot crop is soon injured by autumn frosts. It is therefore advisable to have your main crop lifted before the frosts are experienced. They should be lifted and stored in dry earth or sand, the top being removed and the earth rubbed off, but without any attempt to clean them thoroughly until they are wanted for use.

The wire-worm and the carrot maggot are destructive enemies of this crop. The writer has little faith in nostrums and specifics. Sound judgement as to the choice of ground, deep digging, and preparation of the beds in good time, are the preventives of these as of many other garden plagues. It is often observed that many crops sown early in April suffer more than those sown later in that month, and the lesson is plain. It has also been noticed that where crops have suffered most the land was made ready in haste, and the wild birds had no time to purge it of insects.

The tops from the young and first thinnings can almost be given *ad lib*. Those grown on the larger and matured roots should only be used in moderate quantities, for they soon cause indisposition if fed in excess.

CABBAGES – Although the writer does not recommend this vegetable to be cultivated specially as a crop upon which to feed rabbits, it can be used to advantage by those in whose garden it is grown for domestic purposes. Many fanciers have an objection to using cabbage leaves as green food, mainly owing to the unpleasant smell, which is apt at times to follow their use. This reason is hardly sufficient, however, to debar such an economical and valuable foodstuff. With some fanciers they are about the only green food available during the winter time, and apart from containing a higher percentage of nutritive material than roots, they afford a most valuable change during the open weather.

There are others who are very nervous about using cabbage leaves owing to the mistaken idea that they cause scours or diarrhoea. The writer has never once found them to have been the cause of the least indisposition, especially when used with discretion, a liberal supply of hay being provided at the same time. If you are short of other green food during mid-winter, and find your stock tiring of other foodstuffs, such as roots, have no hesitation in using a cabbage leaf now and again as a tempting morsel. Your rabbits or cavies will appreciate the change. Should any of you have the good fortune, or misfortune, of having a colony of wild rabbits in the vicinity of your garden, you will find that cabbages are not the last greens to be nipped off by the intruders should they have access to your domain; and, after all, nature's lessons are worth taking careful note of.

Some rabbit keepers, I know, make a regular practice of leaving the stumps or stalks in the ground after the cabbages have been cut off to enable them to gather, at a later time, the tender green shoots that grow from the top of the stalks left in the ground. Cabbage stalks, themselves, need never be thrown away as worthless, as when split up into strips they provide still further valuable foodstuff, and, like the stalks of cauliflowers and brussels sprouts, help to keep your stock contented during the time they are nibbling at them, instead of, maybe, gnawing at the woodwork of their hutches.

CELERY – Although this particular vegetable is never grown expressly for rabbit food, many people grow it for domestic use; and I would here remind my readers that a good deal of what is considered waste, so far as human consumption is concerned, can be used to advantage in the rabbitry.

When a head of celery is taken up and brought into the kitchen the first thing you do is to cut off the green tops and then strip it of its outer stalks. The uninitiated would simply consign the latter to the rubbish heap, but not so the rabbit keeper. From the celery trimmings he will be able to provide his stock with a few useful titbits. The green tops and outer stalks can all be used as feeding-stuff for bunny, and are much appreciated when given as an 'extra'. They should always be well rinsed in water to clean off the soil before being given to the stock. Any leavings of celery that come from the table should always be used up as rabbit food.

CLOVERS – This particular green or fodder plant is too well known to need any description. It is a most valuable foodstuff, very nourishing, a splendid conditioner, and a most useful plant to include in a mixture of green food. If you have only a small or limited space of land I don't recommend you to cultivate it specially, as it can be bought in bulk very cheaply. If, however, you have the land available, it is quite a different matter, as a large plot of either red or white clover is a very useful proposition and will keep you well supplied with an abundance of valuable green fodder to cut at.

It is best sown in the early spring on land that has been well cleaned of perennial weeds, as the ground cannot be subjected to cultivation while it is under this plant; and if a little rye-grass seed is mixed with it at sowing time so much the better. Some people sow a mixture of half and half, others three parts clover and one part rye-grass. It can be sown in a generous manner in drills or rows, as near as 15cm (6") between them. After sowing, the land containing the seed should be lightly rolled.

Clover hay is also one of the richest of albuminoids of its class, and if of the first crop and of good quality it is more valuable than meadow hay. A lot depends, however, upon the time of cutting and how clover hay is made. Second crop clover hay is full of hard stalks, and is, therefore, not considered nearly so good as a first crop cut. The one thing to be observed is to harvest it in dry weather, as if the weather is wet it is very liable to become mildewed or mouldy, and if fed in this condition would bring disastrous results to your stock. Good clover hay is sweet in scent, a rich brown in colour, and full of flowers showing colour.

There are several species of clover to be had, but the differences in feeding value are so slight to hardly warrant more than a passing allusion. You will always experience most satisfactory results if your stock have an abundant supply of good clover hay fed to them during moulting time, and whether you harvest your own clover hay or purchase it, keep it in a dry storage when a truss is brought indoors for use, as when it is placed in a damp building it mildews very quickly, and in that condition it is absolutely worthless as food.

DANDELIONS (*Taraxacum officinale*) are too well known to need description. At one time they were practically the only wild green food given to rabbits, and even today they are greatly used. It may surprise many of my readers to note I am treating it under the heading of Cultivated Crops to be grown in the garden. Many gardeners look upon this plant simply as a weed and a nuisance, to be destroyed on every occasion. Others give serious thought to its cultivation and esteem it as a component to a salad owing to its wholesome medicinal qualities. Rabbit keepers can be well advised to reserve a little space upon which to grow this useful green. For preference choose a bed situated in some odd corner or at the end of your garden, as when once the roots become firmly established they provide a permanent crop.

Nature teaches us the way to grow this plant, for she sows the seed in early summer, and we usually find the finest plants on dry ground, while there are, practically speaking, none to be found in bogs or swamps. If you wish you can select the poorest part of your garden on which to grow dandelions. Neither does it matter if your land is gravelled or chalky.

Sow the seed in a small bed at about the beginning of June, and when the young plants are large enough to prick out, remove them to their permanent quarters. If you plant them in rows do so 22cm *(9")* apart, leaving the same distance between each row. They will soon take root, and when once established grow very quickly and afford several cuttings throughout the year until the end of October, when rapid growth ceases. They will grow quickly again in the following early spring, and the older the roots become the larger and more abundant leaves do they grow.

Dandelions have a good tonic effect on the stock, and should be given every other day mixed with other greens, so long as they are available. You obtain the best results in this way, as although they are a safe green food, the writer does not recommend you to feed them in large quantities day after day without any addition of other greens, as owing to being diuretic they may possibly increase the action of the kidneys to such an extent that would not add to the animal's well-being. Dandelions, therefore, you will gather, have a distinct and beneficial effect if fed in reasonable quantities, but, like many other useful foods, they lose their properties if fed to stock in excessive quantities.

KOHL RABI *(Brassica oleracea cauld rapa)* – This vegetable has only to be better known by fanciers to become a first favourite with them. At the present time it cannot be termed a really well-known vegetable in this country, because we can almost always command a ready supply of swede turnips, but on the Continent it is otherwise. There it can be seen in almost every market and on many a good table, where it proves most acceptable. I have always esteemed it very highly as a food for rabbits, and much prefer it to either swedes or mangolds, having grown it for many years with splendid results. It has been most noticeable to the writer that any animal that can eat a turnip will show a marked preference for kohlrabi.

Although it has a similar flavour to a good sound swede, its taste has a somewhat nutty flavour, and it will not scour even the most delicate animal if used with discretion. It is highly nutritious, and no fancier will ever regret using it. There are two varieties, the purple and the green, and it is the latter I would advise you to grow, as it can be successfully cultivated on any ordinary land.

Dig over and prepare your land as you would do for turnips. Sow the seed in shallow drills or rows about 45-61cm *(18-24")* apart, about the middle of April. The seed will soon germinate if the weather is fine and when the young plants are about 7-10cm *(3-4")* high you can begin to thin them out, using the thinnings as a safe green food for your stock. Leave the strongest-looking plants about 15cm *(6")* apart in the rows, thus giving those left a better chance to develop.

In a week or two after this you will begin to notice them 'bulge' out near the top of the stem, just below the top leaves, as the plants become stronger and more vigorous in growth. When they have reached this stage you can go over them again, this time taking out every other two plants and leaving one, so that by the time you have made your final thinning out those left will be

46cm *(18")* apart in the rows. These can then be left standing until you begin to use them in the autumn. Being hardy, they will stand, as a rule, to be pulled as required right through the winter until the following spring. As a winter food for rabbits they are invaluable and much preferred to either swedes or mangolds. Once you have grown and used them you will appreciate their full value.

To those who have not previously seen them they present a unique appearance, being like a green turnip, growing on a short stem and surmounted by a tuft of green leaves. The leaves and the bulb are equally as good as foodstuff. The seed can be bought very cheaply. It should be sown thinly in rows, in a similar manner to that in which you sow turnip seed. If you wish you can sow the seed in a bed, and when the plants are large enough to prick out you can then plant them in rows, allowing a space of 46cm *(18")* between each plant and leaving a distance of 46-61cm *(18-24")*between the rows. I leave the choice between the two methods to the discretion of my readers.

The reason I advise you to grow the green variety in preference to the purple is that the latter is a little stronger and more rank in flavour than the green and not so much appreciated by stock.

KALES – There are several kinds of this valuable green vegetable obtainable, but having given a considerable amount of time and thought to these particular greens, and after a fairly long experience in growing them on various kinds of land and under varied conditions, I consider the Giant or Marrow Stem and the Sprouting varieties are the two most profitable ones the rabbit keeper should cultivate.

The seed of the giant kale should be sown in a seed bed in an open situation about the end of April or the first week in May. Sow thinly in shallow drills or rows about nine inches apart. When the plants are large enough to handle it is advisable to plant them out direct into their permanent quarters, choosing showery weather, or when the land has been moistened previously, for the purpose. Make your rows 76cm *(30")* apart. Then prick out the young plants in them leaving a space of 61cm *(24")* between each, using a wooden dibber for the purpose.

After each plant has been inserted in the ground, press the soil firmly round it with the heel of your boot to make it tight. This enables the young plants to root more quickly, and once they have obtained roothold they will go ahead at a great pace. By the autumn, if they have been grown on even average land, they will have grown stems as thick as a man's wrist and anything from 91-120cm *(3-4')* in height, together with an abundance of side and top leaves.

I leave my readers to imagine how valuable this plant with such a generous growth becomes to a rabbit keeper, especially if he is breeding and rearing on a large scale. Then again, during the period in which his plant is growing to maturity, you can keep going over them from time to time and take off the bottom leaves to use as green food. This does the plants no harm, but, on the other hand, is beneficial, as it enables the stem to thicken a little more quickly through not having the side leaves to feed or support. By the time autumn has arrived, if you have followed this method of stripping, you will have left a plantation of thick stems each surmounted by a green-leaved head. You can then pull up the matured stems, cut off the roots, and chop up the stalks into chunks, and you will then see the results of your labours. And what a joy it is to behold your stock enjoying the sweet nutritious chunks of Giant Marrow Stem kale when feeding time comes round.

When they are large enough some people will prick out the young plants between every other early potato row, after the latter have been banked. Although, if your garden space is limited, you can obtain a fair measure of success by this procedure, I have always found the best results and the production of more robust stems occur if you prick out the plants on land unoccupied by any other crop. I always prefer to plant them out on a piece of land that has been reserved for the purpose, and which has previously been well dug and manured, because a free summer growth is really needful to the formation of a stout productive stem.

We now come to the other variety which has an entirely different habit, as its name, ie Sprouting kale, denotes. The seed should be sown in the same manner and under the same conditions as the Giant variety, only in this case it should not be planted on land occupied by any other crop, such as early potatoes. Strictly speaking, it should have a piece of land previously dug and manured, if possible, in readiness to receive the young plants when ready to be transferred from the seed bed.

These should be planted out in the same manner as Giant kale, ie 61cm *(2')* apart in the rows and 76cm *(30")* between each row.

Sprouting kale does not develop such a thick stem as the Giant variety, but, instead, develops a great number of side sprouts that spring out along the full length of the stalk on much the same lines as brussels sprouts grow. The only difference is that kale sprouts do not 'button' firmly, but possess an open or branching habit. When they become a useful size they can be broken off and used as green food. In time another crop of sprouts grow from the old stem to take their place. Owing to this characteristic the term 'perpetual kale' is often used. The old stalks can be left in the ground, and they will continue to supply you with cutting after cutting of tender, nutritious sprouts of green stuff. Frost will not harm them, and they will stand throughout the winter and furnish you with a further welcome supply of green food in the early spring.

At this time of the year, instead of sowing the seed of this plant you can propagate by breaking off the new shoots close to the stem of the parent plant, and setting these in the ground in the same manner as you had planted out the seedlings in the previous early summer. They, in turn, will grow into sturdy parent plants supplying you with a continuation of sprouts. Another very important thing to bear in mind is that the kale family are not subject to the garden pests that usually attack so many other cultivated greens. Neither are they troubled with fly and other vermin. They can, therefore, be termed a very clean plant as well as a wholesome one.

Apart from being a useful rabbit food, the tender sprouts are much appreciated in the kitchen as a vegetable for human consumption; and the sprouts that mature in the early spring arrive at a time when other garden greens are very scarce or noticeable by their absence. The only drawback, if you can call it such, is that when kale is sprouting it is rather acrid, and has a tendency to make stock a little thirsty.

Sprouting kale also grows a quantity of large stalk leaves as well as sprouts. These are a safe green food which can be fed to both youngsters and adults. Never once have I noticed the least sign of indisposition when stock have been fed on either Giant or Sprouting variety of kale.

LUCERNE *(Medicago sativa)* or **ALFALFA**, as it is sometimes called, is one of the most useful green fodder plants you can grow. It belongs to the well-known leguminous family. When once established it will endure great droughts, its roots penetrating very deeply into the ground, and it always does best in rich calcareous soils. It never succeeds on damp soils or tenacious clays. It is a perennial and affords good crops for a number of years from the original sowing.

The seed should be sown thinly in drills or rows about 30cm *(12")* apart, during the middle of April, on land that has previously been dug over deeply. The first year it should be cut once – just before it begins to flower in the early autumn. The following year and thereafter it affords several cuttings during the year, and if kept free from weeds will be productive season after season for a long time.

In very cold districts it should not be cut down too closely in the late autumn, when you make your last cutting, but should be left with a good top, or the newly-cut plants may die of cold and from want of protection during a severe winter.

The seed can be bought very cheaply, and if you have the land to spare a good bed of Lucerne will provide you with a useful supply of green fodder. I have advised you to leave a space of 30cm *(12")* between each row for the reason that a space of this distance enables you to walk between them if at any time you find the weeds are beginning to gain the upper hand, a state of affairs which if it remains unchecked will soon ruin the whole crop by choking it out.

Lucerne is another safe green food, and one much enjoyed by stock as a change of diet.

LETTUCE – The outside leaves of this vegetable need never be wasted, as a leaf or two now and again is much appreciated by all adult stock and is especially valuable to does that are rearing a litter. It should, however, be used with caution when youngsters have just been weaned and until they are three or four months old.

MANGOLDS (*Beta maritime*) – This is distinctly a root crop and the varieties in cultivation are either globular or oblong in shape, and red, orange, or yellow in colour. The Golden Tankards and Long Reds usually have the best feeding value, but a good deal also depends upon the precise strain and method of cultivation. The Orange and Yellow Globes are perhaps the most commonly grown, owing to their being the most suitable for almost every class of soil. The seed should be sown thinly in rows, the latter being at least 61cm *(24")* apart. The best time for sowing is towards the end of May. When the young plants are large enough they should be thinned out to a distance of about 61cm *(24")*. The matured crop is usually ready to be taken up by the end of October. If left much later it is liable to be injured by severe frost.

The tops or leaves are wrenched off by the hand, and the earth is merely roughly taken away from the roots, as they do not keep so well through the winter if cut or bruised. The roots should be stored in pits or clamps, covered with straw and a little earth, as a protection in severe weather.

The roots when first pulled are also very unwholesome and very liable to cause scouring, for in the autumn and early winter the juices, being unripened, have a laxative effect on all animals. This harshness, however, wears off after they have ripened in the 'pits' or 'pies'. It is usually about the end of January or the beginning of February before they are generally used as food for stock. At this time of the year they are relished by all animals, but they must be used with caution by rabbit and cavy keepers, as apart from their fattening qualities they are not, even when ripe, entirely free from a tendency to a purgative action.

The field mangolds differ from the garden varieties chiefly in being larger in all their parts and coarser.

Mangolds, or wurzels, as they are often called, are so popular with many people because they are liable to fewer diseases and vastly more productive under liberal treatment than turnips, and they come in very useful in the early spring when turnips have little or no feeding value.

It is rather interesting to note that mangolds as a field crop were introduced into England as far back as 1786. At first so little was their value known that the leaves alone were used as food for cattle.

The question of the usefulness or otherwise of mangold leaves as green food for rabbits has often been debated. My own opinion is that they should be used only very sparingly and not at all if you have other more useful greens to choose from.

Sugar beet is a variety of mangold selected for its high percentage of sugar, which in a good strain may exceed sixteen per cent. It is more susceptible to frost than ordinary mangolds, and is a crop I should not advise my readers to grow specially as rabbit food.

PARSLEY (*Petroselinum Crispum*) – This is one of the best-known culinary herbs, and as almost every garden contains a bed of this particular plant it may be of more than passing interest if I devote a little space to its mode of cultivation.

Parsley, like many other good things, will grow almost anywhere and anyhow, but to make a handsome crop, rich, moist soil is required. This, however, does not debar those who have only an average quality of soil from producing a good crop of this particular herb provided they use a little thought.

Nature will teach those who have eyes exactly how it should be grown. There will appear here and there in a garden stray or 'rogue' plants. No matter how regularly the hoeing and weeding may be done, a stray parsley plant will appear alone – perhaps in the midst of lettuces, cauliflowers, or onions. It is rather singular that when these 'rogues' escape destruction they become superb plants, richly curled and sumptuous specimens, proving that isolation suits the plant. The lesson to those who wish to grow parsley is obvious: it should have plenty of room from the very first. This lesson cannot be too often enforced upon all who wish to grow it successfully. As a general rule most people sow parsley far more thickly than is wise, and they appear to be injuriously slow and timid in thinning the crop when the young plants are crowding one another.

To obtain the best results sow the seed thinly in rows or lines that have been made about 30cm *(12")* apart, and when the plants are strong enough to handle thin out to 7cm *(3")* apart and finally to 15cm *(6")*. Should your soil be productive of exceptionally strong plants of very robust growth you can then with advantage allow the final thinning to be as far apart as 22cm *(9")*. When the plants have become well established you can continually keep going over them, plucking off the outer leaves. When parsley has stood some time and you find the leaves become coarse, young growth can be obtained and renewed by cutting the whole plant down. The same operation is useful to defer the plant from running to seed. By continual cutting, a bed of parsley may thus be prevented from running to seed, and it may last several years from the original sowing. If once this development is allowed to mature the whole bed becomes useless, and it should be dug up immediately to make room for a more useful crop.

The leaves of parsley are stimulating and nutritious, and these qualities derive from an essential oil present in every part of the plant. When once the seed stems begin to appear the useful properties of the plant begin to decline. It is rather interesting to note that the seeds are a deadly poison to many birds.

Many fanciers have a very high opinion of parsley as a food for rabbits, and I can safely recommend its use, only, like many other stimulating greens, it should be used sparingly and with discretion at all times. It is an excellent stimulant for stud bucks or does backward at coming into season. Apart from being useful as a green food for rabbits it also supplies many useful purposes in the kitchen. Who among my readers is not acquainted with the ever popular parsley sauce?

PEA HAULM – This need never be wasted, as it forms a useful food either in its green state or afterwards when it is dried. Many rabbit keepers take great care of it in its latter stage and use it as an 'extra' during the winter time. If mildewed it should never be used either green or dried.

PARSNIPS – These can be used instead of carrots, but they are not much enjoyed by rabbits until the spring. They are hardy and can remain in the ground all the winter.

SAVOYS or SAVOY CABBAGE – One of the safest and most useful winter greens known to the rabbit keeper. For method of cultivation refer to 'cabbages'. It is of great value for the bulk of food it produces as well as for its quality as a table vegetable. Savoys produce an abundance of outer leaves, which should be taken advantage of on every occasion they are available.

SPINACH – Any spare cuttings of this vegetable grown in the kitchen garden need never be wasted, as it is a safe green upon which to feed your stock.

STRAWBERRY – The leaves and surplus runners can be used in moderation. They will often check an attack of scours should you have no other remedy available.

SAINFOIN (*Onobyrchis viciifolia*) – This is another perennial plant and will replace Lucerne as a forage crop on poor and chalky soils, arid and burnt by the sun, and of no great depth. It is sown in the spring, and is treated in much the same way as lucerne. It will stand many years if it is not allowed to become choked with weeds. Like Lucerne, it is at its best as regards feeding value if cut before coming into flower. I have referred here to sainfoin because it may prove a useful crop to grow should you have possession of land that is suited to its growth. It does not matter how poor and chalky your land may be; in fact, this kind will be more suitable for growing sainfoin than would be a rich deep loam. If you can grow it successfully it will prove a valuable forage crop with very useful feeding properties, and it can be safely fed to stock of all ages. For method of sowing etc., refer to 'Lucerne'.

SUNFLOWER (*Helianthus annuus*) – It may surprise many of my readers to find I have included this plant as a most useful rabbit food. Although a few fanciers may know its value, a far greater number would pass it over as useless. The species are numerous, it being a genus of plant that belongs to the order compositae, as will soon be recognised by a brief glance at the formation of the flower. They are large herbaceous plants with opposite *(or sometimes alternate)* undivided leaves.

The variety I have selected for description in these pages is the one that is known to almost every individual, ie the annual sunflower that is so common in our gardens.

This variety is a native of tropical America, where it sometimes attains a height of 6m *(20')*. The stem is thick and rough, the flowers solitary and from 30-61cm *(12-24")* in diameter, the leaves being heart-shaped and ovate. This plant is now cultivated in almost all parts of the world, and in the south of Europe it is sometimes seen as a field crop, the seeds being valued as food for cattle and poultry. They yield a very large percentage of oil which is said to be little inferior to olive oil.

The variety now under discussion is, as its Latin name *annuus* denotes, an annual plant – that is, of one season's duration. Although it does not grow in these islands to the same dimensions as it does in the country of its origin, it is, nevertheless, very robust in growth, much on the same lines as the Jerusalem artichoke, which is another member of the same genus.

A simple method of cultivation as well as an effectual one is to make the spot intended for them very rich, and dibble single seeds an 2.5cm *(1")* into the ground, about 45-61cm *(18-24")* apart during the first week of May. The plants will soon begin to appear and make rapid growth. They will eventually be surmounted by a very large disc-shaped flower that grows to an exceptionally large size. It is the flower head that when matured contains a very large number of the well-known and valuable seeds. These when ripe should be collected and kept in a dry place. They form a most useful article of diet during the winter for all adult stock, especially does nursing a litter, should you practice winter or very early spring breeding, as most fanciers do nowadays. A dozen seeds every other day is the usual amount per head given to adults. The seeds should be crushed or bruised, and they are best used along with meal mashes Crushed sunflower seeds, or ones with the husks removed, are enjoyed by cavies and the oil contained in the seeds is beneficial to the guinea pig's coat. If fed separately, some rabbits (not all) may refuse to eat them until they become familiar with them. Owing to the large percentage of oil they contain, they should not be given more generously than I have here advised.

SWEDE TURNIPS (*Brassica napobrassica*) – I now come to the best known and certainly the most used of all root crops. In fact, during the winter season they seem to be the fancier's 'sheet anchor'. This variety is easy to cultivate and can be used for feeding as soon as the roots are pulled at the end of October or the first week in November. They keep well in storage if protected from severe frost, and can be used to advantage up to about the end of February. After that time, unless of exceptional quality, they begin to deteriorate; and once they begin to wither or become pithy they are useless as food. Under no consideration should they be used once they have arrived at this stage.

The principal sowing for winter use should be made during the early part of June. Sow the seed thinly in rows that are about 61cm *(24")* apart if you can allow the room. Should your garden space be limited, you can reduce the distance between the rows to 45cm *(18")*. The best method is to sow the seed after the land has been moistened by showers, as this encourages quick germination and a more rapid growth of the young plant from the seed leaf to the rough leaf stage. This quick growth during the early stage of its existence is very desirable, as it is during the seed leaf period that it is attacked by that well-known pest, the turnip fly. Once the rough leaves make their appearance the danger from this pest can be considered over. My own experience has been that swedes grown in a garden are less liable to an attack of turnip fly than those grown in the field.

When the young plants are large enough to handle, they should be 'singled' to a distance of 30-45cm *(12-18")* apart, according to the room you have at your disposal for growing them and, as with the majority of other root crops, the more room you give them to develop the most robust growth you obtain.

As soon as the crop begins to bulb it is advisable to proceed down the rows with the hoe and destroy the weeds that so quickly make their appearance.

On the approach of winter a certain portion of the crop should be lifted and stored. When doing this the tops must be cut off, not too close, but just leaving a slight green neck, and the roots should be shortened rather than removed. At all events, to cut the roots off close is bad practice, as when so treated the bulbs do not keep well.

Any rough storage answers for turnips, the object being to keep them firm and hard, by excluding the atmosphere, and at the same time render them free from frost. Medium-sized bulbs are better than very large ones, and fed in correct quantities they afford one of the cheapest of the bulky winter foods and are eagerly devoured by rabbits once they have developed a taste for them.

When intended for storage swedes should always be pulled before the first severe frosts come. They should have the tops cut off and the roots ended, as I have advised, being then allowed to lie in heaps for a few days to sweat. When the earth left on the roots has become fairly dry they can be taken in and stored. If you are short of indoor storage room the bulbs can be placed in clamps or 'pies', as they are sometimes called, and so long as they have protection from severe frost they will take no harm.

When feeding rabbits or cavies with turnips during the winter it is always advisable to feed them liberally with hay at the same time. It is also wise to introduce all root crops gradually at first instead of suddenly, especially after the animals have been fed for months on green food. The writer has always made a practice of introducing them to stock along with a little green food at first, just before the latter becomes unobtainable in any quantity. I may also add that the thinnings of young plants make safe and useful green food at the same you 'single' them, and these need never be wasted, as they all form part of the 'grist that comes to the mill'.

TARES or VETCHES are extremely valuable to grow if you have the necessary land at your disposal. Winter vetches can be sown in the autumn to provide green-stuff in the early summer, or summer vetches can be sown in March or early April for use about five or six months later. They do well on heavy land and should be cut for feeding when in bloom, or earlier, as they deteriorate rapidly in digestibility when the seeds begin to ripen in the pods. The last two weeks in September or the first week in October is the best time for autumn sowing.

Tares or vetches should be sown in drills about 15-22cm (6-9") apart, and not any nearer if you wish them to be a self-supporting crop.

This concludes the portion of my book devoted to cultivated greens and root crops. Whatever size garden you may possess, or whatever kind of land you have to cultivate, I am sure you will find something from the selection I have given that you can grow to advantage and which will provide you with ample food upon which to feed your rabbits or cavies. By a careful study of the various individual subjects that have been dealt with you will, by a little careful thought, be able to grow a succession of crops that will provide you with ample food for your rabbits throughout the whole of the year. Seasons may vary, methods of cultivation may differ, but taking this chapter as a whole, I trust it will prove helpful to all those for whose benefit it has been written.

* *Due to EEC regulations several of the varieties mentioned may only be available from specialist heritage seed suppliers.*

USEFUL WILD PLANTS

3

I have now arrived at the part of my book which I hope will prove of special interest to all my readers, ie a short study of the various useful wild plants that abound in every district of our countryside. They are nature's gifts bestowed freely and ungrudgingly upon all who care to take advantage of her bounties.

In some cases they may be regarded only as troublesome weeds growing in a garden, in other instances they may usefully constitute the composition of a grazing pasture; they may adorn the banks and roadsides of our highways and by-lanes, or, maybe, help to form the carpet of verdure that covers hillside or common, woodland or dell, with their luxuriant growth of green. In whatever part of these islands my readers may dwell, from John o'Groats to Land's End, they may be able to gather some or other of the edible wild plants which I shall refer to and on which they can feed their stock.

I fully realise at the outset how impossible it will be within the limits of this book to deal with all the wild plants that are useful as green fodder, and for that reason I shall devote the space at my disposal to those plants and herbs that are most likely to come within the reach of all my readers during their walks through the countryside.

It is not the privilege of every fancier to possess a garden wherein he can grow all the green food so necessary to the health and well-being of his stock. Green food they must have in plenty, especially during the early spring, summer, and autumn, and if this cannot be grown under cultivation, the only course open to the town-dwelling fancier is to make frequent excursions into the country to obtain what he requires. In following this course he not only obtains a free ration for his stock, but benefits personally by enjoying the pleasant recreation of taking an evening walk or cycle ride into the country when his day's work is over. A great many fanciers look forward to this recreation, especially if they have been confined to either workshop or office while following their daily occupation.

It is my intention in the following pages to help my readers to become better acquainted with many useful wild plants that maybe they had no idea were of any value as green food, and thus enable them to make a wider selection than they have previously been in the habit of making. To make my work in this direction more instructive as well as more interesting, I include photographs that should prove of additional benefit to those who require the necessary instructions and knowledge.

For the convenience of readers I deal with my selections of useful wild plants in alphabetical order. Although I shall try so far as possible to avoid technical phrases, a great deal of valuable information regarding medicinal properties would be lost should I be too brief or narrow in my descriptions.

The following definitions of some technical terms should be of assistance:-

ANNUAL
A plant that lives but one year or season once the seed has germinated.

BIENNIAL
A plant that lasts but two years.

PERENNIAL
In botany a plant is called a perennial that lasts over two years from the first sowing, or one that comes up year after year from the original sowing, provided always the root is left undisturbed in its original situation. A great many wild plants have this habit.

ASTRINGENT
Binding or opposed to laxative; a medicine that contracts the tissues and checks discharges.

ANTI-SCORBUTIC
Employed to purify the blood.

APPETISING
Used to promote an appetite.

CARMINATIVE
Soothing.

DEPURATORY
Employed to purify the blood.

DIURETIC
Increasing the action of the kidneys.

EMOLLIENT
That which relaxes and softens the tissues.

LAXATIVE
Having the power of loosening the bowels.

PECTORAL
Employed to afford relief in maladies of the respiratory organs.

RESOLVENT
Employed to improve the condition of sores.

STERNUTATORY
Producing sneezing.

STOMATIC
Favouring digestion.

SUDORIFIC
Employed to induce perspiration.

VERMIFUGE
Employed to prevent or cure maladies due to the development of parasitic worms in the intestine.

AVENS (*Geum urbanum*) – Sometimes known as common avens, wood avens or herb-bennet. There is no mistaking this plant once you have seen it. It grows in hedge bottoms, thickets, or on bank sides, and has the same habit as our cultivated garden flower, the Geum, to which family it belongs. It has dark green leaves and makes its appearance in early spring, thus forming one of the earliest green plants available. Later in the year there appears a long stem which eventually is tipped with a small flower having a narrow band of yellow petals. When the petals fall a small round brownish centre is left in the place of the former flower.

This plant is a perennial, is self-supporting in its habits, and helps to form a useful and safe green to mix with others at a time of the year when many more useful plants have yet to make their appearance in any quantity. It is an astringent and thus a useful herb by which to counteract scours. At one time it entered into the composition of beer in the north owing to its tonic and aromatic properties.

AGRIMONY (*Agrimony euphatoria*) – The only British species – a slender herbaceous plant, one to two feet high. The leaves are pinnate, with the alternate leaflets smaller, and all are deeply cut. The flowers are yellow and grow in long tapering spikes. The whole plant is covered with soft hairs, and when bruised it emits a slightly aromatic scent. Its properties are both tonic and astringent, and on this account it is often collected by village herbalists and made into tea. It is common in waste ground and can also be found growing on the roadsides. Flowering in July and August, it is also a perennial. Although agrimony is not usually recognised as a green food suitable for rabbits or cavies by the average fancier, there is no need to be at all nervous should a small quantity be gathered along with other greens, as owing to its tonic and astringent properties it will not scour even young stock.

BRAMBLE (*Rubus fruticosus*) – or **BLACKBERRY** – A plant too well known to need any description. The leaves of the common bramble are a most useful antidote to scours, and many a valuable rabbit, especially a youngster, has had its life spared by the timely use of bramble leaves when an attack of scours has been first observed.

BURNET (*Poterium sanguisorba*) or **COMMON BURNET** is a most valuable fodder plant and one that should be taken advantage of at every opportunity. It is a perennial plant, and although it grows wild in many parts of England, especially on chalky soils, it has been cultivated owing to its usefulness as a fodder plant. It forms a great part of the natural pasturage of the South Downs, and of the excellent sheep walks of Salisbury Plain, even to this day. The leaves are slightly astringent and are safe to use as green food for stock of all ages.

CARROT, WILD (*Daucus carota*) – Sometimes known as 'earth nut'. A tough-stemmed, bristly plant with much cut leaves, having large umbels of dull white flowers, the centre flower or partial umbel being bright red or deep purple. In flavour and scent it resembles the garden carrot. It grows abundantly in pastures, flowers in July and August, is a biennial in habit, and is a safe plant to use as green food. This must not be confused with Wild Beaked parsley, which is a dangerous plant.

COW PARSNIP (*Heracleum sphondylium*) or **HOGWEED**, is one of the most valuable wild plants used by rabbit keepers. It makes an early appearance all over the countryside, growing on every hand in the lanes, hedgerows, banksides, and pastures, and is a free-growing plant of a robust nature. It should be used on every occasion, as large quantities can be gathered in almost every part of the British Isles. When the seed stems appear they grow to a great height, giving the plant a very robust appearance. Its stems are channelled or grooved on all sides and are to be found both green and of a reddish purple in colour according to the conditions under which it is grown.

In the spring this plant is remarkable for the large oval tufts formed by the sheathing base of the centre stem leaves, which contain the flower buds. Cattle seem to be able to eat this plant with impunity, and it is a wholesome and nutritious food for small livestock as well as cattle. It is also very succulent and particularly useful for does nursing a family of youngsters. The writer has used this particular wild plant for many years, having found it most beneficial and absolutely devoid of any detrimental or harmful properties.

Country people are very fond of calling it humlock and thus it becomes confused with the poisonous hemlock. It is an entirely different plant from the latter and need never be mistaken owing to its coarser and less cut leaves. Cow parsnip or hog weed begins to flower about July and is most conspicuous then all over the countryside, and it need never be mistaken. After it has begun to flower, however, the leaves and leaf-stems only should be used, as the flower stems are apt to be rather indigestive if given to young stock. You need never be afraid of hogweed causing scours even in young rabbits. The flowers are of a creamish colour, sometimes being tinged with a pinkish shade. They grow in umbels – or like an umbrella in shape.

COMMON COMFREY (*Symphytum officinale*) – This is another wild plant that has often been the subject of much discussion. A great many rabbit-keepers know it quite well, but have been rather doubtful as to its usefulness as a fodder plant. Let me here and for always dispel any doubts, as the common comfrey can be safely used as a green food. It is a large, handsome plant, 61-91cm *(24-36")* high, of robust growth, and has large coarse leaves. It is a very common plant which grows in watery places and on the banks of streams. It is a perennial, and the flowers *(white, pink, or purple)* droop in forked clusters. This plant will never cause scours if given to the most delicate rabbit owing to its astringent properties. It is nutritious and flowers May and August.

CLOVERS (*Trifolium*) – Another green food plant that needs no description, as it is so well known to all. It can be found growing among the short grass of almost every roadside and in most pastures. There are several distinct varieties all of which have either white or deep pink flowers, and all are excellent when used as green food. It is a plant rabbits never seem to tire of, and when mixed with grass it forms a most valuable green fodder.

COLTSFOOT (*Tussilago farfara*) or **TUSSILAGO**, as it is often called – The flowers of this plant usually appear during the very early part of the year. The flower stalks springing directly from the roots are covered with scale-like bracts, and each stalk bears a single flower, yellow in colour, having numerous yellow rays or petals. The leaves, which do not appear until the flowers have withered, are heart-shaped, being a medium shade of green on the surface. The underneath part of the leaf is of a silvery shade or colour, being covered with a cottony or down-like substance. The Goldfinch frequently lines its nest with the pappus of this plant.

It is a common plant found in many gardens and on arable land, and is difficult to eradicate once it becomes established. The leaves are fleshy in substance and the roots grow to a great depth, and also shoot out in all directions. The latter are very brittle, and the least bit of one when broken off will commence to grow another plant. Coltsfoot is a safe plant to use and makes a welcome change when mixed with other greens. It can often be found growing on land where potatoes are cultivated, and if left undisturbed the leaves grow to a very large size.

CROSSWORT (*Galium cruciata*) or MAYWORT, as it is sometimes called, need never cause you any alarm should a little be found in your green meat bag after you have been out on a 'gathering' expedition. I have often given this plant to stock along with other greens and have always found that my rabbits enjoy it.

It is a very common plant of a perennial habit which can be found growing on almost every bank side or in hedgerows along the lanes of our countryside. It derives its name from the formation of its leaves which are on a slender stalk. They grow directly opposite to each other in fours, forming a cross, and they occur in this manner at short intervals all the way up the stalk. It is an upright plant, and the tiny pale yellow flowers which emit a fragrant scent, appear just where the base of the leaves join the stem. There is no mistaking this plant when you take a walk along the country lanes during May and June, as you are met on all sides by the fragrant and unmistakable scent that its tiny flowers emit.

CLEAVERS (*Galium aparine*), also known by the names of cly, sweetheart, and goose grass, belongs to the same family of plants as crosswort, although of an entirely different habit. Cleavers is not a self-supporting plant. It commences to grow on the top of the banks near the bottom of the hedge, and before the season has very far advanced it will have grown to the very top of the hedge that it relies upon for support. Should it be found where no support is at hand by which to help an upward growth, it will run along the ground for a long distance. The stalks are square and are very rough, and they stick to the fingers when touched.

The round seed-vessels are also very tenacious and disperse themselves by clinging to the coat of any animal that touches them, hence they derive their popular name of cleavers. Children are fond of gathering and throwing them on to the clothes of their companions, to which they easily cling, hence the name sweetheart.

Geese and turkeys are very fond of this plant and eat it greedily, and in many parts of the British Isles it is known by no other name than goose grass and turkey weed by country people. It is an exceedingly common plant and flowers in June, July and August. The round seed balls naturally follow, and I don't suppose there are many of my readers who, after having a ramble in the country during the autumn, have not found some of these clinging to their garments.

Cleavers is a safe plant to use, and many fanciers who know of its medicinal properties, give it to stock when they first notice they are at all laxative. When this plant is in its seed stage it is rather troublesome if given to Angoras, as the tenacious seeds become embedded in their wool and their removal is difficult. With a little care, however, this can easily be avoided.

CHICKWEED (*Stellaria media*) or **COMMON CHICKWEED** – A plant only too well known to everyone who is fortunate enough to possess a garden. Its leaves are egg-shaped and grow in pairs all along the slender stem. A peculiarity about this little plant is a hairy line that runs up one side of the stem. When this reaches a pair of leaves it then continues on the other side of the stem and so on until it reaches the top of the plant. It spreads very quickly, when once established, and soon becomes a nuisance to the gardeners. Chickweed cannot be termed a valuable green food, but as it is safe to use, a little makes a welcome change when other greens are scarce. It is an annual and can be found in flower almost the whole year round. The flowers are very tiny and white in colour.

DANDELION (*Taraxacum officinale*) – The common dandelion is another plant that needs no description. It is well known by every school-child. It is a valuable green food that has a tonic effect, and a little mixed with other greens should be used every day when available. I would here warn my readers against using it in large quantities day after day, as by so doing harmful results may accrue. Dandelion used in large quantities and not mixed with other greens may eventually prove too laxative as well as diuretic, and thus cause irritation to the kidneys. Yet when used in moderation it proves a most valuable green food to stock of all ages. It is rather interesting to learn that the name dandelion is from the French *dent de lion* (lion's tooth).

DOCK (*Rumex obtusifolius*), or **BROAD-LEAVED DOCK** is too well known to need any description. It makes a very early appearance in gardens, pastures, lanes and on cultivated land. Although not generally recognised by fanciers as a green meat, this plant has its own usefulness, as rabbits thoroughly enjoy its leaves, especially in the early spring after they have been fed for a long time on roots. The tender young leaves can be safely used as one of the first spring greens, and being astringent they make a useful green to mix with grass etc when first introducing green food to your rabbits in the early spring. Later in the year, when the seed stems begin to appear, the plant deteriorates in food value, and as other greens become more plentiful you can discontinue using dock.

DOCK (*Rumex crispus*), **CURLED DOCK**, is another variety of this genus, and is almost as common in some parts as the common dock. It is easily distinguished from the latter by its acute curled leaves from which it takes its name. It can be used along with the other variety to advantage, and at the same period of the year. Curled dock is reputed to contain iron and is also an astringent plant.

DOCK (*Rumex acetosta*) **SORREL DOCK**, often called **SOUR DOCK** – The most useful of all the docks: it is a very common plant, being abundant in meadows. It is well known for the grateful acidity of its herbage. The leaves and stems, being of a juicy nature, are appreciated and eaten with a relish by all stock. The leaves are arrow-shaped, and easily recognised from those of other docks.

The flowers grow in whorled spikes, are of a reddish green colour, and are carried on stems from 22-61cm *(9-24")* high according to the strength and robustness of the plant. These to the casual observer look like a mass of seeds in appearance, but a closer examination will soon prove to the contrary. The leaves of this plant help to form a useful mixture of green food and can be used with safety and fed to stock of all ages.

GOUT WEED (*Aegopodium podagraria*), **COMMON GOUT WEED, BISHOP WEED, GROUND ELDER ETC** – A very common weed that makes its appearance in the early spring, helping to form some of the first green titbits for stock. I always use a little of this particular plant, mixed with other greens, during the early part of the year now and again as a change. I can safely recommend it when fed in this way. It is a perennial, umbelliferous plant, and now a very common weed to be found in gardens and on waste or uncultivated land. It is thought that this plant was originally introduced into Britain by monks from the Continent on account of the virtue ascribed to it of allaying pain in gout etc. Its medicinal virtue is, however, now discredited. It is still used in Sweden, I believe, until this day as a pot-herb when the leaves are young. Once the seed stems begin to appear I should advise my readers to discontinue its use. Before it reaches the latter stage of growth it is slightly stimulant and can be used with safety as advised to stock of all ages.

GROUNDSEL (*Senecio vulgaris*), also known by the common name of birdseed – A plant that is found growing in almost every garden, and which, if used with discretion, is of great value to the rabbit keeper. Its leaves are of a ragged appearance and dark green in colour. The flowers grow in clusters, small in size and pale yellow in colour, and these when having reached the seed stage are like tiny dandelion blooms, excepting that they grow in clusters (instead of single flowers) on a single stem.Groundsel grows to *7.5*-30cm*(3-12")*.

The plant begins to bloom when only a few centimetres in height, and as it continues to grow it throws out side shoots, each of which are tipped with a cluster of small flowers. Although I have given a short description of this particular plant, I suppose there are few of my readers (especially those who possess a garden) who are not fully acquainted with it.

Its medicinal properties are laxative and stimulating, and for this reason it has long been recognised as a valuable food to give to stock during moulting time, as it helps the rabbit considerably to have a quick, clean moult. If a particular individual should 'stick in the moult', a little groundsel given each day along with other green food will very often have the desired effect. Nothing is more irritating to the rabbit keeper than to find his or her stock begin to moult and stop when about half-way through. The above little tip should be borne in mind should you experience the trouble referred to. It can also be used in the ordinary way as green food, and stock usually appreciate a little now and again mixed with other greens.

When gathering you should be careful to avoid any plants attacked with an orange-coloured fungus. This is very noticeable, even to the most casual observer, and if a very little caution is used it need never be overlooked. The fungus referred to is a parasite and may prove of detriment when in its active stage. You may go for months and never find a single plant attacked by the pest referred to. In that case, all is well. Yet, on the other hand, you may come across almost every plant infested more or less by it. If such be the case, avoid it. I simply refer to this in passing, being anxious to omit no detail, however small, that I feel sure will be for the benefit of my readers.

Groundsel should never be fed to stock in large quantities day after day without a change, owing to its laxative tendency, but when used as advised it is of considerable value. It is an annual plant and can be found in flower almost the whole year round.

HEATHER (*Caluna vulgaris*) – This well-known order contains a large number of plants, many of which are remarkable for their social nature, extensive tracts of country being often found entirely covered with a few species. This gives the name 'heaths' to the kinds of places on which they grow.

Although common heather is not generally recognised as food for rabbits by the town-dwelling fancier, those who live in the districts where it abounds are well acquainted with its usefulness, and frequently make use of it as fodder. It is a safe plant to give to stock, so those who have it available need never be at all nervous about using it. It is another plant having astringent medicinal properties.

Wild rabbits feed upon it a great deal, and it is reputed to give a palatable flavour to their flesh. Its flowers are a favourite resort of bees, and the seeds and young tender shoots enter largely into the food of moor fowl.

HAWK BIT and **HAWK WEED** are an order of wild plants containing a great many different varieties. It will be of little use describing each single variety in detail, as to the casual observer they differ very little. Some of the more common kinds are also known by the name of segrum. This family of plants can all be used along with other greens as safe food for rabbits. They are a very common plant found growing in lanes, on bank sides and pastures, in almost every district of the British Isles. The leaves in appearance are very similar to the common dandelion, except that they are rougher in substance and of a more slender nature in appearance. The flowers are of a bright yellow colour, borne on long, slender stalks, and in formation are very similar to dandelion blooms. In fact, the whole appearance of the plant is like a slender dandelion. In some pastures they grow in abundance, it being difficult to avoid them even if you wish.

COW PARSLEY (*Anthriscus sylvestris*) – This graceful plant is one of the first green herbs to make its appearance in the very early spring. In fact, if the weather is unusually mild, a nice gathering can be made from sunny situations even during the month of February. Owing to it being procurable so early in the year, it is much appreciated by stock after they have been fed for several months during the winter on root crops.

This is one of the most discussed green foods used by rabbit keepers. Many fanciers, especially new beginners, are a little uncertain about using it owing to its close resemblance to both upright hedge parsley and the deadly hemlock. A little explanation, however, should soon remove my reader's doubts. For one thing, cow parsley makes its appearance much earlier in the year than both hemlock or wild beaked parsley. The latter have also round and smooth green stems of a very bright shade of colour, whereas cow parsley has a ridged, branched hollow stem, almost V-shaped in appearance. There is no need to confuse hemlock with cow parsley, as the former is most noticeable by having its stems or stalks covered with purple brown blotches or round patches of this colour, giving them an almost spotted appearance. Cow parsley is altogether devoid of these markings, and if this plant is found growing in open situations the leaf stems are of a deep pink or purplish shade of colour, especially when you observe the lower part of the stalks. This shades off gradually to a pale green as you come towards the fern-like leaves at the top of the stem. The leaves are very much cut (or pinnatifid, as they are called in botany), and in appearance are very much like a fern to the casual observer.

This plant is a perennial in habit and can, therefore, be found coming up year after year in the same situation. It flowers during the early summer and onwards until the end of August, and can be found growing in all situations. Although used in moderation and along with other greens it is a safe and harmless plant to give to adult stock, it should be used very sparingly when fed to young stock after just being weaned, and on no occasion should youngsters have it given to them *ad lib*, or without other green food. Once the seed stems begin to show the flower buds it is advisable to stop using it, or, at least, only the leaves and leaf stems should be given to stock. Like many other wild plants, it serves a useful purpose when fed in moderation, but if given to stock in large quantities, without any additions, it may prove unsatisfactory.

The flowers are of a creamish colour and grow in umbels, almost like an umbrella in appearance, large numbers of tiny blooms being massed together, thus forming a round and nearly flat-shaped top, which, when seen through the microscope, have a decidedly beautiful appearance.

IVY (*Hedera helix*), **COMMON IVY** or **CLIMBING IVY** as it is frequently called, needs little or no description, and can be found growing in hedgerows in almost every part of the British Isles. Rabbits are very fond of ivy leaves, and seem to be able to eat them in the winter time with impunity. I should not advise my readers to use them except in the winter or very early spring. In the late summer and early autumn this plant should be carefully avoided, as at this time of the year the flowers, followed by the fruit of the ivy, appear. The latter is both purgative and emetic, so I think I can leave the use of ivy leaves safely to my reader's discretion, especially after this brief explanation. In early spring and winter it is useful. In summer and autumn, when at the flowering or fruiting stage, it is best left alone.

KNAPWEED (Family *Compositae*) – There are two varieties of this commonly known plant, both of which are safe and useful green food, ie great knapweed (*Centaurea scabiosa*) and black knapweed (*Centaurea nigra*). The latter is the more common variety, and as it is the most likely to come before my reader's notice I will confine my remarks to it.

This plant is popularly known by the name of hard-head, and is to be found growing in great profusion on bank sides in our country lanes. It has a pinkish purple flower, not at all unlike our common thistle in shade and shape. In fact, to the casual observer the flowers of the black knapweed, seen from a distance, may be mistaken for a light purple thistle flower, excepting the blooms of the knapweed grow on long, slender, single stalks that are absolutely devoid of prickles. The bottom part of the flower looks just like a blackish-brown ball, and this is surmounted by the delicate-coloured petals. The stalks, though slender in appearance, are very tough and grow from 30-61cm *(12-24")* high. The leaves are of a light green shade and are mostly found at the base of the plant leaning over toward the ground.

It may be of interest to my Scottish readers to learn black knapweed is called horse knot in that country. This plant can be safely given to stock of all ages, and containing as it does astringent properties, it will not cause intestinal disarrangement of even young stock and helps to form a useful mixture of green food. Some rabbits will eat it greedily, others partake of just a little.

The botanical name, *Centaurea*, has its origin in an ancient legend concerning the cure of a centaur by one of the species. The centaurs (bull-killers) were a wild race of men who inhabited in early times the forests of Thessaly, and whose chief occupation was bull hunting. Homer, who first mentions them, describes them merely as savage, gigantic and covered with hair. The centaurs are celebrated in Greek mythology on account of their wars with Hercules. It is indeed most interesting to learn how some of our plants receive their names.

The black knapweed is a perennial plant, and thus, if the roots are left undisturbed, it can be found growing year after year in the same situation. It is very common in some meadows, and when once firmly established seems difficult of extirpation. It flowers June to August.

KNOT GRASS (*Polygonum aviculare*), commonly known as bird's knot grass, is an insignificant looking weed found growing in large quantities on waste ground or by the roadside, also in meadows. Although not regarded as such by many rabbit keepers, it is a valuable and safe green food, and it is for this reason I bring it to my reader's notice.

It has long, tough stalks to which are attached tiny leaves. These grow in pairs. Where they are attached to the stalk a 'knot' appears. Should you care to take the trouble of stripping the leaves from the stalk, the latter will have the appearance of a piece of closely knotted string. When this weed is found growing on waste ground without other plants to support it, the stems, which are branched, lay prostrate along the ground, but if found growing in a meadow it has an upright habit and appears erect, partially supported by other taller grasses etc., although by habit it is not a climbing plant. The flowers are very tiny. They are flesh-coloured and are also to be found of a greenish-white shade. These appear just at the base of the small leaves where they join the knotted stem. Further description seems unnecessary as a glance at the illustration will be quite sufficient to show you its character and appearance.

It is a very valuable green food, and stock seem to enjoy it at all times. Care should be taken to see that it is not covered by dust, especially if gathered from the roadside. This can easily be overcome by rinsing it in a bucket of clean water. The same process can and should always be practised with other greens if gathered in dry or dusty weather. Knot grass is an annual plant, but owing to the numerous seeds it grows and shakes it can be found growing season after season in the same place, as the seeds easily germinate.

MALLOW (*Malva sylvestris*) or COMMON MALLOW – This plant is one of a very large order or tribe, ie the mallow tribe. According to Lindley, the number of species hitherto discovered amount to about a thousand, all of which agree in containing a large quantity of mucilage, and being totally destitute of unwholesome qualities.

The particular specimen I wish to describe is the common mallow, a plant that is common enough in a great many districts, on roadsides, in by-lanes, waste ground, and it is sometimes to be found growing on bank sides and in meadows. The leaves are kidney-shaped, with seven acute lobes, and they appear massed together at the base of the flower stalk, which grows erect from the centre of the root crown. When the flowers, which are of a showy pinkish-purple shade, first expand this plant has a particularly handsome appearance, but as the season advances the leaves lose their first deep green hue and the centre flower stem puts on a ragged appearance. The stem then is nearly bare, with just one or two leaves appearing here and there upon it.

Common mallow is a very safe plant, and no ill-results will ever occur from its use.

NIPPLEWORT (*Lapsana communis*) or **COMMON NIPPLEWORT** is a safe and valuable addition to the green food menu. It is a leafy plant often found growing to a height of two to three feet. It is common in hedgerows and waste ground and is also found growing in great quantities in many gardens as a common weed. When it first appears on cultivated garden land the base leaves spread out almost flat on the ground. Although usually of a delicate shade of pale green, they are often found tinged with a light brownish tint of colour. The centre flower stem is slender, branched, and grows to a height of anything from one to three feet, according to the conditions under which it is grown. The flowers are very small and of a pale yellow colour. They are similar in shape (only very much smaller) and shade to the dandelion bloom.

This particular green food should be used whenever the opportunity occurs, as rabbits thoroughly enjoy it at all times. It is an annual plant and can be found in flower any time from July to the end of September. The young weeds begin to make their appearance early in the spring, and even in the north of England I have made useful gatherings of fair-sized plants before the end of April.

PLANTAIN (*Plantago major*), or **GREATER PLANTAIN**, is one of the most commonly used green foods. It is well known for its long spikes of seeds, which are also a favourite food for cage birds. The leaves of the greater plantain are, broadly, egg-shaped, and grow on long channelled stalks. The flower or seed stalks very often reach a length of 30cm (*12"*), half of which is covered with the seed capsules. No further description is needed, as a brief glance at the illustration will suffice.

Large quantities of this useful plant can be found growing on the borders of fields, country lanes, waste places, and on cultivated land. Those specimens that abound in the ordinary garden are of a more delicate appearance than those found on arable land, and the seed stems are also proportionately smaller.

This family of plants forms a very useful green food, and all rabbits and cavies derive benefit from its use. It is not laxative in its action, and will not scour the youngest of stock, even if fed to them in large quantities. In fact, all plantains are slightly astringent in their section.

PLANTAIN (*Plantago lanceolata*); also known as long-leaf plantain, ribwort plantain etc – Under the name of cocks and hens this plant is well-known to children, who amuse themselves by striking the seed heads one against another until the stalk breaks.

Although long-leaf plantain belongs to the same family of plants as the broad-leaf variety, the former is entirely different in appearance. Its leaves, as the Latin name denotes, are lanceolate, or long and narrow, and it is also ribbed along the full length of the leaf. The flower or seed head is short and grows long, angular stalks. It is found growing abundantly in meadows, bank sides, and country lanes, and its good properties as green fodder are well known. It is encouraged by the farmer in all permanent pastures, and is even sown among clover and other seeds on seed fields.

Long-leaf plantain is a perennial plant. It is slightly astringent in its action, and should be taken advantage of and fed to stock of all ages whenever the opportunity occurs. When mixed with green clover and grass it forms a very useful rabbit and cavy food.

SHEPHERD'S PURSE (*Capsella bursa pastoris*) or **COMMON SHEPHERD'S PURSE** – A common weed, to be found in almost every part of the world, varying considerably in luxuriance, according to the soil and situation. In hard, stony ground, it grows only a few inches high, but in rich soil as much as two feet high. The root or base leaves are pinnatifid or cut; those on the stem are cut near the base where they join the stalk, but toward the end are uncut and taper toward the tip. It is an annual plant flowering nearly the whole year round. The flowers are white in colour and very tiny in size.

A brief glance at the illustration will convey at once to my readers' minds what to look for in their search for this truly valuable plant, so further description on my part is unnecessary. I would like to draw attention to the formation of the seed pods. These in appearance are like a small purse, hence the name shepherd's purse, or money-in-both-pockets, as it is called in some districts.

This weed has long been recognised as a real 'fancier's friend', and one that is first thought of when stock is attacked by scours. It is both tonic and astringent in its action, and many a valuable rabbit has been saved when shepherd's purse has been given on the first symptoms of scours having made their appearance. The whole part of the plant can be used – root, stalk, leaves, seeds and flowers. When given in this way, all that is necessary is to rinse the entire plant through clean water to wash off the soil from the roots and base leaves.

When gathering this weed be careful to note that no white fungus is attached to the stem. Sometimes you will find it very prevalent. Avoid all plants so affected. You may go a long time and never find it at all. The fungus referred to is easy to notice, as it is like a fine white powder clustered around one or more parts of the stalk. With a little caution such specimens can be easily avoided. Shepherd's purse can be fed with benefit to stock of all ages at all times and seasons, and the animals enjoy it.

SOW THISTLE (*Sonchus oleraceus*), or **MILK THISTLE** as it is often called, is one of the best-known wild green foods procurable. It has for generations been eagerly sought after by fanciers, and used whenever the opportunity occurs. It is an erect, branched plant and very often attains a height of 120cm (*48"*). When the stem is broken a milk-like juice immediately appears, giving it the well-known name of milk thistle. A more valuable green food I cannot recommend to my readers, especially for does nursing a family. It is safe to give to stock of all ages. This plant must not be confused with the common prickly thistle, which is useless.

Sow thistle is easily distinguished from the common thistle by its bright yellow blooms, which are very similar in shape and colour to the dandelion flower. These appear in clusters at the extreme top and branches of the plant, and there is no mistaking them once you have seen them. There are several varieties of this weed, all of which are equally useful. Some have perfectly smooth, tender leaves, while others are slightly prickly, but not in such a way that will cause either inconvenience to the gatherer or when eaten by stock.

These plants are most useful when fed while the stalks are tender and juicy. When fully grown the bottom half of the centre stalk has a tendency to become hard and 'woody', and unless your rabbits are very hungry they will avoid it. The plant is at its best when about one foot or two feet high, and it is at this stage of its growth I recommend it. It is an annual plant, found growing in waste places, and is also very common as a garden weed. It flowers June to September.

TREFOIL (*Trifolium*) – This family contains a great number of distinct varieties, many of which are recognised as first-class green food. In appearance they resemble miniature clover and are very common in dry pastures. The best-known variety is *Trifolium minus*, or lesser clover. Its leaves resemble shamrock, and the flowers are similar in composition to the well-known common clover. They are, however, very much smaller in size and of a pale yellow colour.

It has a creeping habit, and in many districts is very common, and large quantities can soon be gathered in a small area. It is a valuable food in its green state, and equally good when dried. Meadow hay containing a large amount of trefoil is regarded by all stock-keepers as a prize indeed. Rabbits appreciate this plant either green or in its dried state and eat it greedily. I strongly advise my readers to take full advantage of it whenever the opportunity occurs as it is safe to use when fed to stock of all ages.

VETCH (*Vicia*) or **TARES**, as they are commonly called, belong to a genus of plants of the natural order *Leguminosæ*. The species are mostly climbing plants, annuals, with pinnate leaves ending in tendrils, and with no terminal leaflet. They are found growing on bank sides in many districts. In others they form the chief ornament of hedges and bushy places in the latter part of summer.

Vetches are not a self-supporting plant. If growing on bank sides, they trail along the ground, or else rely upon what little support they can derive from the herbage among which they grow. When growing near bushes or hedgerows, they climb upward, clinging to the supporting object by means of delicate tendrils, in much the same manner as our cultivated garden peas have the habit of doing. They have usually red or purple flowers. One variety, the meadow vetch, is conspicuous from the others owing to its yellow bloom. The wild vetches all grow pods, which contain the seeds, and when they arrive at this stage they look like a miniature garden pea. Wild vetches are a useful and safe green food, and, those who live in districts where they abound should make full use of them.

WATERCRESS (*Nasturtium officinale*) needs no description. The leafy shoots are very tasty, and a rabbit 'off colour' can often be tempted to eat this well-known green when all others fail. The whole plant is a useful stimulant for the stomach, being depurgatory and anti-scorbutic. When at its best I am afraid little will find its way to the rabbitry, as it is a plant very much appreciated on the table. This plant is in its prime before the flowers appear. After it has reached the latter stage it is useless. It is an aquatic plant, being very common in clear running water, where the best specimens are obtained.

YARROW (*Achillea millefolium*), also known by the name of milfoil. This is a common roadside plant with very tough, angular stems, which sometimes grow to 30cm *(12")* high. The flowers are small, and many of them grow together in a cluster. To the casual observer they look like a single flower. They vary in colour from white to a pale pink.

The whole plant when bruised emits a distinctly aromatic odour. The leaflets are much cut into hair-like segments, and a brief glance at the illustration will no doubt make further description unnecessary. This plant can also be found in most pastures, where it is always encouraged. It contains valuable tonic properties, and is often sown along with grasses to help form a permanent pasture.

DANGEROUS PLANTS, SHRUBS, & TREES TO BE FOUND IN FIELD & GARDEN

4

I think it will be the better plan to divide this chapter into two parts – Part I to deal with those dangerous plants that you may find growing in their wild state; Part II to deal with dangerous plants, shrubs, and trees that are to be found under cultivation, or in the garden.

I would like to remind my readers that when describing as poisonous certain of our wild plants, or those to be found under cultivation, it must be borne in mind that the word 'poison' is a purely relative term. Many plants etc described as poisonous, come under that heading because certain properties they contain are deadly when in their concentrated form as prepared by chemists. Others are of a much more dangerous character even when given in only small quantities. Take, for example, the common sorrel dock. Children have been made ill by eating too many leaves of this particular wild plant. Most of us as children, especially those who have been brought up in country districts, are well acquainted with the pleasant acidity of this plant which we know by the name of sour dock. It is also perfectly harmless as a salad plant, yet its pleasant acidity is due to the presence of binoxalate of potash, which when sold as salts of lemon is a dangerous substance.

Any substance of a definite chemical composition, whether organic or mineral, may be called a poison, if it is capable of being taken into any living organism, and it causes by its inherent chemical nature impairment or destruction of function. Other plants that are termed as poisonous are not always as bad as they are made out to be, and here I would quote the lines of our great national dramatist, Shakespeare, who wrote:

> *'There is a soul of goodness in things evil;*
> *Would man observing distil it out.'*

Thus a large number of substances, very poisonous if taken in quantity, become valuable medicines in the hands of skilful practitioners.

Although this book is purely one for the use of rabbit keepers, I cannot refrain from stating that it would be beneficial to all children if our county clergy, schoolmasters, and schoolmistresses knew more about wild flowers, so that they could distinguish between poisons and harmless plants and thus impart that knowledge to the younger generation under their care. The number of children who are made more or less ill by eating berries, leaves etc., which are to be found in the fields and hedgerows, is undoubtedly very considerable every year, and even though the number of fatal results may be very small, a good deal of indisposition could be prevented had those who are responsible for the teaching of children the necessary knowledge referred to. It is not merely children who should be warned against putting anything they find growing wild into their mouths, as even adults are often apt to make the most stupid mistakes.

The garden aconite, which no one can mistake when in flower (it having long been cultivate in cottagers' gardens), has been the cause of the death of whole families. In the gardens of country people, a little horse radish is often grown. In the winter the roots of aconite have frequently been dug up and given to a family in mistake for horse radish, and fatal results have occurred. Town dwellers, who have changed their abode for a country residence, have been known, through ignorance, to mistake the leaves of fool's parsley for the true parsley, and such a mistake, although not proving fatal, has caused painful results.

PART I

To deal with all the dangerous wild plants contained in the *British Flora* is impossible in a book of these limitations, so I will confine my remarks to those which my readers are most likely to find during their excursions when looking for wild green food for their rabbits and cavies.

ARUM (*Arum maculatum*); also known by the common names of cuckoo-pint, lords and ladies etc – This plant makes its appearance early in the year. In sunny situations it is often to be found in new leaf by the end of February. It is usually found growing on bank tops, near the hedge bottom, or in sheltered situations of orchards. It is well known by its leaf, being shaped like an arrow-head, and often spotted, and the large sheathed spathe with the purple spadix, which bears the male and female flowers upon it.

The flowers give place to berries, which by the early autumn will have become a bright red. These form a cluster at the end of a short upright stem. All parts of this plant, tuber, leaves and berries, are poisonous. Many cases are on record where children have died after eating the berries.

ANEMONE (*Anemone nemorosa*); also known by the name of wind flower – This is one of our most beautiful spring flowers, adorning our woodlands at the season when primroses and violets are in perfection. The flowers are generally white, but they are not infrequently tinged with pink externally. More rarely they are of a delicate sky-blue from within and without. Cattle have been poisoned by eating the wood anemone in the fresh state, after having been underfed and kept on dry food during the winter. Under those conditions many animals become less discriminating and ready to eat any fresh green food that comes their way.

The flowers of the anemone are similar in shape to those of the buttercup. The leaves also are not unlike those of the latter plant, excepting that they are finer in build.

AUTUMN CROCUS (*Colchicum autumnale*); also known by the common name of meadow saffron – This plant is frequently found growing in meadows in many parts of England. It is well known by its rose-coloured flowers, resembling those of the crocus, hence it has been called meadow saffron or autumn crocus, but it has no relationship to the crocus it so closely resembles. This plant flowers in the autumn, and the leaves do not appear until the following spring.

All parts of the plant are poisonous. Drying does not remove the deleterious property. Water in which the leaves and flowers are macerated becomes very poisonous. Animals have been poisoned by eating the leaves when they have grown among the grass of a grazing pasture. Children have also suffered the same fate after eating the bulbs they have found in the fields. The Turks are said to use an infusion of the flowers in wine to add to its inebriating effects. A peculiarity of this plant is that at the time of flowering the seed vessels are concealed beneath the ground, where they remain until the following spring, when they rise above the surface and are ripened.

BUTTERCUP (*Ranunculus*) – This plant is too well known to every child or adult to need description. Although there is a deleterious principle contained in nearly all kinds of ranunculaceae, the ordinary common buttercup cannot be termed a deadly poison, and although I advise my readers to avoid it as much as possible, no harmful results would occur should a little become mixed with other green foods, when fed to either rabbits or cavies. If given to stock in large quantities and not mixed with other greens, it would cause harm. Buttercups are perfectly harmless when dried in hay.

BLUEBELL (*Scilla non-scripta*) or **WILD HYACINTH** – Common throughout the British Isles, and needs no description. The bulbs are very acrid, the deleterious principle residing in a viscous juice which appears to pervade the whole plant. Avoid this plant always when green gathering.

BELLADONNA (*Atropa belladonna*); also known as the deadly nightshade – This is a perennial herb, between three and four feet in height, having a branching habit. The flower has a tubular corolla of a purplish-blue colour. The berries that follow the flower are rather large and of a shining black colour when ripe. Belladonna is very poisonous, the berries, which are intensely sweet, having caused many mishaps among children. The roots contain the most active principle, the stem, leaves and flowers coming second, and the berries third. Drying will not destroy the poisonous properties.

Men and animals suffer alike from the belladonna, but in different degrees. Man is most susceptible. After him are the cat, bird and dog. The horse is less affected by it. Pigs, goats and sheep are but little sensible to the actions. It is rather interesting to learn also that our friend bunny is also but little sensible to its action, probably in consequence of a more rapid elimination of the poison.

I remember once reading an interesting account of belladonna causing disaster to some troops under Mark Antony. This was described by Plutarch, who said that those who sought herbs obtained few that they were accustomed to eat, and in tasting unknown plants they found one which caused insanity and death. Those who had eaten of this plant immediately lost all memory and knowledge, but at the same time would busy themselves in turning and moving every stone they saw, as if they were engaged in some very important pursuit. Plutarch states that the camp was filled with unhappy men bending to the ground and digging up and removing stones, till at last they died after bilious vomiting, when wine, the only remedy, was not at hand.

This noxious plant, which is one of the most dangerous growing in Britain, on account of its active poisonous properties, is, fortunately, of rare occurrence, growing principally in old quarries and among ruins. I once read a statement to the effect that rabbits could eat the leaves of belladonna with impunity to themselves, though it rendered their flesh dangerously poisonous for human food.

BLACK NIGHTSHADE (*Solanum nigrum* is a smaller plant of a branching habit. It is very seldom found growing much over a foot high. The leaves are egg-shaped, wavy at the edge, and bluntly toothed. The flowers are white, with yellow anthers, in drooping bunches. The berries are globular, black or sometimes of a dull red. This is an annual plant found growing on waste ground, although I have seen it growing freely in neglected flower and vegetable gardens. The flowers you will observe from the photograph are not unlike the white flower of some varieties of our cultivated potato.

BRYONY (*Bryonia dioica*) or **WHITE BRYONY** is an elegant climbing plant, with large light green, rough leaves. This plant grows in great profusion, completely smothering the hedges upon which it climbs. The flowers grow in bunches and are of a greenish-white colour, with darker green veins. The fertile flowers may be distinguished at once from the barren by the presence of an ovary below the calyx. These develop into globular scarlet berries, which hang in clusters about the hedges long after the stems and leaves have withered. The plant itself is less injurious than the berries, the latter being poisonous. The illustration of this plant will also save any further description. It is a perennial, and a nuisance once it becomes established.

BRYONY (*Tamus communis*) or **BLACK BRYONY** is another familiar climbing plant, found scrambling over hedges upon which it relies for support. The leaves of the black bryony differ greatly from those of the white. They are glossy, of a darker green, oval and pointed. The flowers are very small and of a green colour. The sexes are also distinct on different plants, and all bear large quantities of scarlet berries in the autumn. The foliage of this plant is also less dangerous than the berries. The poison in the latter class has been proved to belong to the acrid narcotic class. Taken in smaller doses than are sufficient to cause death, the berries of the black bryony cause paralysis of the lower extremities.

BINDWEED – This family of climbing plants is well known, and although they cannot be termed as being deadly poisonous, I should not recommend them to be used as green food for rabbits or cavies in a general way. One species I would, however, draw your attention to, ie the black bindweed (*Polygonum convolvulus*). It is very common in cornfields, the stem climbs up the stalk of wheat etc and apart from its flowers this plant closely resembles the lesser bindweed (*Convolvulus arvensis*). When the seeds of the black bindweed are too much mixed with oats it has been found that after a considerable period serious internal derangements follow. Polygonums are bitter and rich in tannin, but they are not otherwise known to be poisonous.

Should a little of the lesser bindweed become mixed with your ordinary green food no really serious results would follow, as this variety is not poisonous, or even dangerous, except when the seeds have become developed. During the seed time all bindweeds are best avoided.

The lesser bindweed has small pink flowers streaked with white.

THE GREAT or **HEDGE BINDWEED** (*Catystegia sepium*) is another variety. This is a most mischievous weed in gardens, not only exhausting the soil with its roots, but strangling with its twining stems any plants which grow near. The flowers are handsome when expanded and of a pure white colour.

CELANDINE (*Ranunculus ficaria*), **LESSER CELANDINE, FIGWORT** or **PILEWORT**, as it is often termed, is a plant well known to all country people. The leaves are heart-shaped and of a glossy green colour. It is one of our brightest and earliest spring flowers, studding every bank with its bright yellow, star-like flowers. Children are fond of gathering this pretty flower, which is one of the first to appear. When the plant is young it is less dangerous than when fully matured.

It is also interesting to note that the strength of the acrid principle it contains varies according to locality and season, but I recommend my readers to avoid this plant at all times and seasons.

CELANDINE (*Chelidonium majus*) – The greater celandine is a totally different plant to the lesser celandine. It is frequently found in hedgerows about villages and stony places. It has much divided leaves, small, four-petalled, yellow flowers, which are followed by long seed pods. This plant is supposed to have been an old medicinal drug plant of the Middle Ages. It was probably introduced at that period and eventually became a naturalised plant in Britain. It exhales a disagreeable odour and is a strong irritant when applied externally. It also acts as a very severe irritant upon the intestinal digestive organs of both humans and animals. A peculiarity lies in the fact that the poisonous principle remains long in the system, so that domestic animals poisoned by it should not be eaten.

It is also known by the name of swallow wort, probably owing to it coming into flower about the time of the swallows' arrival in this country, and the last flowers beginning to fade about the time of the birds' departure in the autumn. The greater celandine contains an orange-coloured juice, which is a violent acrid poison.

CORN COCKLE (*Agrostemma githago*) – This is a common cornfield weed, a tall and erect annual with opposite pairs of long narrow leaves. As the seeds are shed simultaneously with the ripened corn among which it grows, they are apt to communicate injurious properties to the flour. The seeds have no scent but are bitter to the taste. Corn cockle is a plant which no cultivator of land should allow to flourish, as the whole plant is deadly poisonous. Fortunately, very few animals will touch this plant, but at the same time it should be removed from their presence by vigorous destruction at every available opportunity.

DOCKS- These include sorrel dock, common dock and curl dock. All these plants have been included in a previous chapter on useful wild plants. They are useful during the early spring while their leaves are young and fresh, but when the seed stems have appeared and the seeds become ripe, they are best avoided, as although the leaves can still be used they lose a good deal of their feeding value once the seed stems have appeared. The seed stems, however, should always be avoided, as dock seeds contain a dangerous substance known as binoxalate of potash, or salts of lemon, and are very poisonous. My readers should, therefore, always remember that the leaves when young are useful, but during the seed stage the plant is best avoided.

DOG MERCURY (*Mercurialis perennis*) – This plant makes its appearance during the early spring, often covering large patches of ground on the roadsides and banks of our country lanes. It exhales a disagreeable odour, so that animals rarely eat it, except when it is given to them mixed with other herbage. Sheep have been poisoned by dog mercury after they have eaten it in its green state. Heat, however, soon destroys its injurious property, and it is also innocuous when dried into hay.

In its fresh green stage it is a decidedly harmful plant, the seeds are dangerously purgative, and many fatal results following its use are on record. The botanist, Ray, records a case in which a whole family of five persons suffered severely from eating it in mistake for spinach, and two of the children died the next day. Dog mercury certainly does resemble spinach when in its flower stage, excepting that the leaves of mercury are of a much darker green in colour.

ELDER (*Sambucus nigra*) – Common elder is a shrub or tree familiar to all. It grows wild in the hedgerows throughout most parts of this country. Its flat-topped corymbs of numerous yellowish-white flowers is familiar in the late summer to all country people. Elder flowers, which yield a volatile oil by distillation, are used to make poultices etc. The berries which follow the flowers make an excellent wine, and I should say that most of my readers are familiar with elder-berry wine, as it is called. The leaves of this shrub or tree should always be avoided. An infusion made from the leaves is fatal to insects, and many gardeners use a strong infusion to preserve delicate plants from insect pests and caterpillars. The young leaf buds are very purgative and somewhat dangerous in consequence. The bark, too, is violently cathartic, and cases are on record where the leaves have caused severe irritant poisoning in children. Common elder is also known by the name of botrey or botree.

FIGWORT (*Scrophularia nodosa*) is a very common wild plant, mostly found in shady and moist places. The stem is quadrangular (or square). The leaves are smooth and toothed. The flowers are small and of a deep rich red colour. This plant is also known by the common name of fiddlesticks. Country children are very fond of using one stem as the bow and a second one as the fiddle, and when one stem is drawn across the other a peculiar squeaking sound is produced. The plant acts as an emetic and purgative with great energy. Fortunately, most animals will not touch it, and although no case of actual poisoning by this plant is known, I advise you to regard it as suspicious.

FOXGLOVE (*Digitalis purpurea*) – This handsome wild flower is to be found in both field and garden in nearly every county. All parts of the foxgloves are poisonous, but the seeds are richest in the deleterious principle. The leaves are more active before flowering than afterwards. Under cultivation the principle is less active than in the wild plants. Neither drying nor boiling destroys the poison.

Foxglove, or Digitalis, as it is usually called, is so powerful in its action that (as Dr Hogg observes) as a medicine it should never be administered unless by a skilful and practised hand, because of the danger resulting from an imprudent use of it. One of its peculiarities is that after having been given in moderate doses for several days without apparent effect, it sometimes acts suddenly on an accumulated influence, even to the danger of life. To illustrate the folly of ignorant people trying to doctor themselves, I recall reading of a case where a woman, having used the freshly-expressed juice of foxglove for the purpose of relieving swelling of the limbs, experienced much suffering and then died on the twelfth day.

The flowers grow on long handsome spikes, and are usually of a deep pink colour, although white foxgloves are also often met with. In my own garden I have found both the pink and white shade growing side by side. Further description of the plant seems unnecessary, as a brief glance at the illustration will immediately convey it to your mind.

FLAGS (*Iris pseudo-acorus*), **YELLOW or CORN FLAG** – This plant is found growing in great profusion along the water sides of our rivers and lakes, and is well known by its beautiful bright yellow flowers. It has long been known as dangerous, and even Linnaeus states that the iris is dangerous to cattle. All species of iris, or flags, must be regarded as equally suspicious for the flowers, as well as the rhizomes, have drastic properties and also very marked emetic ones.

FOOL'S PARSLEY

(*Aethusa cynapium*) – This poisonous plant is one I particularly wish to draw your attention to, as many people mistake it for both cultivated parsley and hedge parsley. It is an annual weed in both gardens and cornfields. The leaves, which are of a dark green colour, rise from the ground, and when the centre stem appears other leaves branch from it. Both the flower stem and leaf stems are of the same dark green colour as the foliage. The flower stem is channelled, the leaf stems are grooved, and the foliage of the leaves is smoother than that of common hedge parsley. When in flower this plant is easy to recognise. The flowers grow in what are called umbels, and cluster together on little pendicels radiating from a terminal point on longer stalks, which again radiate from the main stem. This arrangement is called a compound umbel. When the flowers of fool's parsley are fully developed little 'beaks' pointing downwards appear underneath them, and this peculiarity in itself makes the plant easy to recognise. The flowers are white in colour, the leaves much cut and pinnate, and the roots are similar to the tap root of the cultivated parsley. Fool's parsley is a plant you should carefully avoid, as it is poisonous to animals, birds and humans. Convulsions and stupor occur in all animals poisoned by it.

HEMLOCK (*Conicum maculatum*) – This deadly poisonous plant has been the subject of more discussion by rabbit keepers than any other weed I know, mainly on account of its foliage being similar to that of common hedge parsley. Then, again, we have that useful plant called hogweed, sometimes called humlock by country people. Humlock, in turn, becomes the subject of further misinterpretation, ie hemlock. Yet the difference between hogweed and hemlock is most marked. The former has a grooved stem and coarse broad leaves, and is altogether different in every way to the latter. Hemlock is a tall biennial, growing from three to six feet or more. It has a forked pale yellow root. The stem is erect, hollow and perfectly smooth. It is bright green in colour, but mottled with stains or spots of port wine colour. The leaves are large, the segments being deeply cut. The 'tooth' or tip of each leaf is tipped with a minute sharp white point. This plant grows in hedges and waste places, and is easily recognised by the above characteristics, especially by the smooth spotted stem. The leaf stems are also smooth, round and spotted, whereas those of common hedge parsley are grooved or V-shaped.

When the stems of hemlock are bruised they emit a most disagreeable odour. The hemlock was well known to the Ancients as poisonous, and it was the juice of this plant, in all probability, that Socrates was compelled to drink. Like so many other poisonous plants, it is much more injurious in the hotter countries of Southern Europe than in the north. Before flowering the poisonous principle is chiefly in the foliage, but it becomes less so when the plant is in 'fruit' or seed. The latter then acquires it, and it is more active before the seeds are ripe than afterwards.

It is worthy of note that when cut and dried, as in hay, the hemlock loses most of its poisonous properties, which are volatile and easily dissipated. Animals are not often poisoned by hemlock, and those who do suffer have eaten it by mistake when it has been mixed with other herbage, more especially in the early spring, when they are prone to eat with avidity anything green.

HENBANE (*Hyoseyamus niger*) – This plant is poisonous in all its parts. It is chiefly found growing on waste ground. It grows about 30cm *(12")* in height, and is densely hairy and sticky. The leaves are large and deeply indented. The flowers are of a yellowish colour and pencilled or veined with a violent tint. The form of the flower is funnel shape. The seeds are very poisonous. The whole plant is characterised by a heavy nauseous odour, and neither drying nor boiling destroys its noxious properties. As a rule, no animal will touch a plant.

Dr Houlton records a case where the whole inmates of a monastery were poisoned by using the roots of henbane in mistake for chicory. Those who partook of the roots had such hallucinations that the establishment resembled a lunatic asylum. They rang the bell for matins at midnight, and those who attended were unable to read, or they read that which was not in the book.

OAK (*Quercus robar*) – The parts of this tree to which I draw your attention are the young leaves and shoots. In early spring, at a time when the new supply of forage has hardly appeared, all kinds of titbits are eagerly sought after by rabbit keepers, and animals that have been deprived of green food for weeks are often given young shoots and leaves of trees. This is a dangerous practice. When the foliage of not only oak, but hornbeam, hazel, furze, and broom is fully matured, they all contain tannin. But this product is perfectly harmless, so the belief at present is that certain substances, which subsequently become tannin, are injurious in that previous condition in which they occur in the young and early spring foliage of various trees and shrubs.

I well remember one of our leading specialist breeders of chinchilla rabbits informing me that hazel leaves were the only green food his rabbits were given for weeks together. But in that case they were matured leaves and not the early young shoots. I give this information to illustrate my meaning that where some varieties of young shoots and leaves are best avoided in their early stage, they can be used to advantage when fully matured.

POPPIES – These wild plants need little or no description. Almost every child knows them by their beautiful scarlet flowers. Some varieties are more dangerous than others, but, taken as a whole, they are best avoided when gathering green food for either rabbits or cavies.

SCARLET PIMPERNEL (*Anagallis arvensis*) – This is too small a plant to be eaten in any quantity by animals, but experiences have shown that it certainly contains injurious properties, which neither drying nor boiling destroys. Before the flowers arrive, this plant might easily be mistaken for the common chickweed. Cage birds have been poisoned by their owners giving them scarlet pimpernel in mistake for chickweed. In appearance it is a pretty little prostrate plant, with tiny bright scarlet flowers, which expand only in fine weather, and this has gained for the plant the name of poor man's weather-glass. There is no mistaking scarlet pimpernel for chickweed when in flower, as the chickweed has a tiny white flower. Scarlet pimpernel once had a reputation for curing hydrophobia, but no such property is now attached to it. An extract made from it is very powerful and poinsonous.

SPURGE FAMILY (*Euphorbiaceæ*) – All spurges should be carefully avoided. The variety most likely to be found by rabbit keepers is the common or petty spurge, also known by the names of milk-weed, cat's milk etc. It grows in abundance in most gardens, but by patient weeding and hoeing it is soon destroyed. It contains a thick milky juice which is acrid and poisonous, and the seeds are also dangerous. The juice of spurges, when applied to the skin, acts as an irritant, and it has also the same effect upon the digestive organs and intestines of rabbits, cavies etc.

It is only by close observation you notice that this troublesome weed is in flower, as owing to the flowers being almost the colour of the leaves, they may easily escape your notice. The seeds which follow the flowers are also green, and not unlike small capers. The leaves are slightly oval in shape, very smooth, and of a beautiful shade of green. It is a small plant, usually found growing about 15cm *(6")* high, and seldom attaining more than about 25cm *(10")* in height. I suppose there are very few of my readers who are not familiar with milk-weed, especially those who have a garden. Immediately you break the stalk the white milky juice appears, and this reference in itself will no doubt soon bring it to your memory.

TOAD FLAX (*Linaria vulgaris*) – In appearance this wild plant is very similar to our cultivated Antirrhinum or snapdragon. It usually grows to a height of 30-61cm *(12-24")*, but the writer has frequently found it in the south of England growing to a height of 91cm *(36")*. The centre or flower stem is well furnished with numerous grass-like leaves, and the dense clusters of pale yellow flowers are like miniature snapdragon blooms. Toad flax is acrid and poisonous. The odour and taste of the flowers prevent animals from eating them. Little is known of their toxic principles. This plant is a perennial, and can often be found growing in dense masses along our hedgerows.

TRAVELLER'S JOY (*Clematis vitalba*) – Also known by the common name of old man's beard. This hedge shrub is common where limestone or chalk enters largely into the composition of the soil. It climbs other shrubs by the help of its twisting leaf stalks, its woody stem and young branches often carrying it to a height of several metres. It is well distinguished in summer by its loose panicles of greenish-white fragrant flowers, and in winter by its tufts of feathery seed vessels, the latter giving it the appearance of an old man's beard.

Some authorities state that its name, traveller's joy, is derived from Gerard's description of it 'decking and adorning ways and hedges where people travel'. It has also been stated that this plant was a favourite with tramps, who used its acrid juice to blister their arms and hands and thus excite pity from those whom they approached for assistance, hence the name traveller's joy. This plant is very acrid and poisonous.

PART II

DANGEROUS PLANTS, SHRUBS AND TREES OF THE GARDEN

Although many of the subjects I shall refer to in this part of my book are well known by name to the majority of my readers, it does not necessarily follow that all will be conversant with their dangerous properties. I feel that my efforts on this occasion would not be complete unless some kind of reference is made to a number of dangerous plants, shrubs and trees that are to be found in almost every rabbit keeper's garden.

ACONITE (*Aconitum napellus*), also known by the names of monkshood, wolf's bane, and granny's nightcap, is one of the most poisonous plants known. This old-fashioned flower has deeply-divided leaves, which to the casual observer may easily be mistaken for those of the Delphinium. The tall spikes of pretty blue and white flowers are also similar in shape to the snapdragon (Antirrhinum). It is a perennial plant, and if the roots are left undisturbed the plant will appear year after year in the same situation.

Aconite was well known to the Ancients as being deadly poisonous, and it was the poison used in the island of Ceos, where all who were of no use to the state were poisoned, and old men were thus disposed of.

All parts of the plant are dangerous – leaves, flowers, and roots. The taste is bitter, and is soon followed by a burning sensation, accompanied by great salivation. So acrid is the poison that when the juice is applied to a wound on the hand it may affect the whole system, not only causing pains in the limbs but a sense of suffocation and syncope.

Aconite poisoning of wells by a virulent Indian species has been carried out by native Indians to stop the progress of an army, as in the case of the Nepal War, but it was discovered in time. It was also used for poisoning spears and arrows for the destruction of savage wild animals. The whole plant is so dangerous that all who have a limited space for their flowers or vegetables should be advised never to grow it, and if it is established in any garden, no effort should be spared in its destruction.

ACACIA (*Robina pseudo-acacia*), also known by the name of locust tree or false acacia – This tree is a very familiar one in many gardens. The flowers, which are white, resemble in form those of the laburnum. The acacia contains a poisonous principle in both leaves and bark.

BEECH (*Fagus sylvatica*) – It may come as a surprise to many of my readers that I should include beech in this chapter. The leaves and twigs of this tree are perfectly harmless, but it is the 'masts' I wish to warn my readers against using. Many people are in the habit of gathering beech nuts and using them as a rabbit food, and although the 'kernels' are safe and can be eaten with impunity, the husks, or 'masts', contain a deleterious principle. Beech nuts have been crushed for the sake of the oil they contained, and the refuse, or husks, have been made into cakes for cattle. But it has been found that they suffer from some very deleterious principle, which appears to reside in the husks alone.

BOX (*Boxus sempervirens*) – Most of my readers will be acquainted with this familiar garden shrub, which is frequently used as an 'edging' for garden paths and around flower beds. This shrub is also used in what is termed topiary work, and trained into all kinds of shapes, such as birds, pyramids etc., which make pleasing ornaments in a garden. It is said that the Ancient Romans introduced this custom.

All parts of the box emit a disagreeable odour and taste, and it is very nauseous. Animals have injured themselves by browsing upon box shrubs, especially in arid districts deficient in proper herbage. Pigs have died after eating the cuttings. The leaves and barks contain the poisonous principle, which is emeto-purgative, and can be fatal in its effects. It is on record that the porcupine is the only animal that can eat box with impunity.

CHRISTMAS ROSE (*Helleborus niger*), also known by the name of Lenten rose. There are two distinct species of this genus. One flowers in autumn and winter (Christmas rose), and the other in spring (Lenten rose). Both are valuable types for garden decoration, because of their flowering during the dull periods of the year. The Christmas rose is perhaps the most popular on account of its pure white flowers being obtainable at Christmas-tide.

Both the species referred to have leathery cut leaves and belong to the buttercup order (*Ranunculaceæ*) – This popular flower is grown in most gardens, and I warn my readers against using it as green food. It was formerly used medicinally, but it has been discarded from the pharmacopoeia as too uncertain and dangerous in its action. The roots are stated to possess the greatest activity, but the leaves are also poisonous.

COLUMBINE (*Aquilegia vulgaris*) – This old-fashioned and popular garden flower needs no description. The whole plant is harmful, but the seeds are the most dangerous. Our present-day 'long-spurred' Aquilegias are the 'improved' columbines.

DAFFODIL (*Narcissus pseudo-narcissus*) – A pretty garden flower, well known to all. The bulbs of the daffodil, as well as every other part of the plant, are powerfully emetic. The flowers also have been known to produce dangerous effects upon children who have swallowed portions of them.

GYPSOPHILA, often called chalk plant – This plant is remarkable for its numerous feathery panicles of small starry white flowers, borne in profusion on threadlike stalks throughout the summer. Most gardeners who grow sweet peas have a bed or border of Gypsophila. These flowers are used to mix with sweet peas for table decoration etc. Cases of ill-effects have been recorded where Gypsophila has been eaten by animals.

HYACINTH (*Hyacinthus*) – A bulbous-rooted and well-known garden plant that needs no description. All parts of this plant should be carefully avoided. The bulbs are very poisonous.

IVY BERRIES – Although ivy leaves can be safely eaten by rabbits, the berries should be carefully avoided. Ivy berries are very emetic and purgative, producing more or less inflammation in the digestive canal.

LABURNUM (*Laburnum anagyroides*) – This is certainly one of the most poisonous of all trees cultivated in gardens. All parts are harmful – roots, bark, leaves, flower buds, pods, and seeds. Drying has no influence upon its poisonous property.

LARKSPUR or DELPHINIUM is another well-known garden plant which I warn my readers to avoid. It is much cultivated in gardens at the present time, and is prized for its beautiful spikes of handsome blue flowers. Larkspurs grow a quantity of foliage, and I have frequently been asked by rabbit keepers if this plant is dangerous, and for that reason I have included it among plants to be avoided.

LILY OF THE VALLEY (*Convallaria majalis*) – This plant is harmful in all its parts, the flowers being most dangerous. Not only lily of the valley, but all garden lilies should be carefully avoided.

LOBELIA (*Lobeliaceae*) – This is a well-known miniature border flower familiar to all. It is generally spoken of and described as blue Lobelia. The Lobelias contain a bitter and acrid milky juice, and are dangerously poisonous. They are often used to decorate garden vases, window boxes, hanging baskets and garden borders.

LOVE-IN-A-MIST (*Nigella damascena*) – This is a well-known old-fashioned garden flower, also known by the name of 'devil-in-a-bush'. The flowers are of a pale blue shade and are surrounded by finely-divided leaves, which form the 'mist' or 'bush'. This plant should be carefully avoided owing to the dangerous properties it contains.

NARCISSUS (*Narcissus poeticus*) – This bulbous plant is extensively grown for its beautiful flowers, which are white in colour and have a beautiful scent. Narcissus, like the daffodil, is frequently grown in orchards, and makes a pleasing sight in the early spring.

All parts of the plant are harmful, and the bulb is said to be even more dangerous than that of the daffodil. Many rabbit keepers make a practice of mowing young orchard grass in the spring time. When this is done, great care should be taken to avoid the leaves of both narcissus and daffodil being collected at the same time.

POTATO TOPS – I am frequently asked if potato tops can be given to rabbits and cavies, and for this reason I have included them among my dangerous plants. Cattle have been known to suffer when potato tops have been given to them at times of scarcity of forage. Potatoes themselves that have been left on the land until they become green should also be carefully avoided.

PRIVET (*Ligustrum vulgare*) or common privet, is a well-known shrub, and privet hedges are very popular in a large number of both town and country gardens. It is an evergreen shrub, which grows very quickly. Rabbit keepers often inquire as to its usefulness. Privet clippings I advise you to carefully avoid.

RHUBARB LEAVES – Many rabbit keepers, when short of green food, have been tempted to use rhubarb leaves as fodder. This has been followed by fatal results.

SNOWDROP (*Galanthus nivalis*) needs no description. This is one of our earliest flowers, and another plant that is frequently to be found growing among the grass of orchards etc. It should be carefully avoided.

SCARLET RUNNER (*Phaseolus coccineus*) – Although this plant supplies us with an excellent and highly nourishing food, I warn my readers against extravagant use of the foliage as green food. It appears to contain some deleterious property, which especially resides in the roots.

TULIP (*Tulipa*) – Another well-known bulbous plant that needs no description. There has been found in the tulip a principle which has been called tulipine, and if it is introduced into the system of either animals or humans in any quantity it would cause harmful results.

YEW (*Taxus baccata*) – This tree is classed among the most dangerous for cattle. It occasions more accidents than others because it has no repelling scent or flavour. Animals are apt to browse upon its foliage, especially in winter. The wood, bark, leaves and seeds are all poisonous. It is the leaves which are most dangerous, and, rather singular, it is the older dark green, and not the bright green spring foliage which is the most harmful. When yew trees or yew hedges have been trimmed, all the clippings should be carefully collected and burnt at once.

The poisonous character of the yew was known to the Ancients. Caesar, for example, mentions the fact that Cativolcus poisoned himself with it. I recall reading an account of some horses being taken to a country fair to be sold. They were tethered to the churchyard railings, over which some yew branches hung. The horses ate the leaves and all died.

This concludes Part II, and although a greater number of subjects could have been included, I have taken those which I consider are most likely to come before my readers' notice, and which are to be found most frequently in the rabbit keeper's garden.

ALLOTMENTS 5

As a country lover living in an urban environment and as a cavy fancier wanting to feed my stock as well and as naturally as possible, I find that the allotment plot is an essential part of my life. It enhances my quality of life, is a quiet haven in a busy world and provides both my family and my stock with fresh produce for the greater part of the year.

In my youth, I bought my first cavy bible, Mice & Cavies by Ralph Blake and here it recommended that "you plant a patch of your garden especially for cavies" and I suspect that this noted writer would have given very similar advice to the rabbit fancier.

Initially, I grew only chicory for summer and spring use but kale is also given special mention in the above book and both marrow stem and thousand head varieties provide good fodder and are a useful addition to the diet in the late autumn, winter and early spring periods. In addition, I do normally grow purple sprouting broccoli for the kitchen and, once the cropping season is over, the leaves and split stems can be fed to stock. Here we have a good example of how gardening and cavy interests can overlap and be of mutual benefit to both.

An even greater dual purpose crop is sweetcorn where the family can enjoy the cobs *(normal or mini-pop)* whilst one's stock will greatly relish the plant itself and the silk and trimmings from the cob. The silk is particularly beneficial as it has medicinal value *(demulcent, diuretic, tonic)* and I am told that it is helpful against urinary tract infections and kidney stones. Of course, you can also feed the cobs to your stock if you have excess and are willing to overlook stocking the freezer for future kitchen needs.

In fact, there are several crops that will benefit the kitchen and livestock alike and although I have read detrimental comments about the use of dwarf and runner bean waste in relation to rabbits, I have never found it a problem with cavies. The kitchen trimmings are shared round the stock and when the dwarf plants have finished cropping, these are fed with the runner vines being systematically cleared in the autumn to provide a regular supply of green-stuff when much of the wild vegetation is dying off.

The chicory *(Brussels Witloof)* is grown specifically for the livestock but there are other varieties *(more lettuce-like in character)* that can be grown for salad use and my stock have never complained about the type grown as long as it is fresh and plentiful.

Fodder beet *(Mangold x Sugar Beet)* is something else grown specifically for my stock as it is usually well received and is non-staining. As a result, it is particularly useful to those keeping light coloured breeds where the feeding of carrots and beetroot is likely to be restricted. Both the leaves and the root can be fed.

The seed should be sown in April although May is not too late but, of course, the shorter the growing season, the smaller the crop. Opinions vary but I sow the seed in 2.5cm *(1")* drills, 45cm *(18")* apart and thin out the seedlings *(they supplement the green bag)* in two stages to around 22cm *(9")* apart. As I can only obtain pelleted seed, I carefully water the drill before sowing to soften the casing around the seed and encourage germination. The crop is ready for use from September into early January. If sufficient is grown it can be fed into the spring if you are prepared to clamp it or make a "pie" *(large hole dug out and lined/covered with straw)*. Many varieties are no longer available but Kyros can be obtained from J.W. Boyce, Bush Pasture, Fordham, Ely, Cambs,CB7 5JU or, alternatively, you may know a friendly farmer.

Carrots and beetroot are enjoyed by the family and stock alike although home grown crops are mainly for the kitchen *(horse carrots being available for most months of the year)* with only the oddments and misshapes being assigned to the caviary. Whilst carrot tops are much enjoyed by most stock, it should be pointed out that beetroot tops should be consigned to the compost heap as they contain too high a level of oxalic acid to be safely fed.

Mention of compost heaps reminds me how complimentary are the hobbies of livestock keeping and gardening as the cleaning out waste from hutches can be allowed to rot down at the allotment with the end product used on the plot when doing the winter digging. In this respect, I am reliably informed that rabbit manure is one of the most valuable with a dry matter content of approximately 2.7% Nitrogen, 1.5% Phosphoric Acid and 1% Potash with only 63.5kg *(140 lb)* of fresh manure required to make 45kg *(100 lb)* of dry matter. However, values are likely to vary according to the bedding used and you will find that hemp based products *(e.g Hemcore)* decompose much quicker than wood shavings and, likewise, hay or barley straw will break down faster than wheat straw.

Most weeds can also be composted although, at this point, I must confess my love of weeds as the majority such as sow thistles are of great value and are best fed to stock. They are a free food available simply for the trouble of collection. In addition, some are a benefit to the wildlife that assist the organic gardener and I have a small clump of yarrow that will, hopefully, attract lacewings.

However, a word of warning here. Although, dandelion seed can be bought from some seedsmen/herbal outlets and may well be catalogued as "Excellent for salads, has medicinal properties. Helps to keep everyone young", a magnificent crop of it will not exactly find favour with your fellow allotment-holders. It may be readily accepted by stock but it should not be fed in excess because of the plant's diuretic properties. That said, I rate dandelions well above lettuce *(contains laudanum)* and I only bother to feed the latter if really nice and I'm short of feed content. In fact, I know of rabbit rescue people that have declined lettuce for their inmates even when offered free.

Of course, the benefits of allotment-holding are much more than simply a supply of fresh vegetables as the allotment site will prove to be a community in itself and the whole exercise can be an escape from the stresses of modern life and a real aid to one's well being. In this regard, whether the allotment site is council or private owned, it is probably a good idea to join or form a local group and affiliate to the National Society of Allotment and Leisure Gardeners of Hunters Road, Corby, NN17 5JE. This organisation helps maintain green lungs within the urban landscape and provides one with a seed order scheme at discounted prices.

Allan Trigg

Greenfoods

for Rabbits & Cavies

by F R Bell F.R.H.S.

with additional chapters by Allan Trigg

Fur & Feather
Incorporating Rabbits

COMPOSTING

These days we are being encouraged to reduce, re-use and recycle. All for the sake of the environment and the fact that landfill sites are running out.

Hopefully, we can all do our bit to improve matters and composting the cleaning out waste from our stock will certainly re-use and recycle into a useful product that, otherwise, would be rubbish for landfill. Also, I compost as I find it rather gratifying to get something beneficial for virtually nothing.

All vegetarian animal waste can be composted along with other organic waste from the garden or kitchen. There are a few exceptions; mainly anything diseased (that should burnt) and it is not advisable to compost some weeds e.g. couch grass (twitch). Weed seed should also be avoided.

For anyone without livestock, a wormery or the plastic dome-like containers offered by local councils will do a good job but these lack the capacity for anyone keeping rabbits or cavies and having waste in bulk. One can simply have a heap on the ground but it is better to make two box-like constructions out of pallets or corrugated iron sheets. The reason for having two units is so one can keep new waste separate from older maturing waste. When well rotted and ready for use, this will then not become mixed up with the latest additions.

The contents of a compost heap should be kept moist to allow decomposition and this can be accelerated with the addition of stinging nettles (before going to seed) and comfrey leaves are also very beneficial. Adding soil is helpful too as there will be mini-bugs and other micro-organisms that will assist with the composting operation. Otherwise, you can purchase Garotta, a proprietary product for this purpose but I have never found the need. Although not essential, it is recommended to cover the heap with sheeting to retain the moisture and this will also discourage foxes from searching for worms.

At this point, it should be mentioned that there are two approaches to composting; aerobic (where the heap is regularly turned to allow access to air) and anaerobic (without air and where the heap is simply left untouched to decompose slowly). With a fairly balanced supply of water and oxygen (assisted by the micro-organisms), the former should generate more heat and be more expedient. Those of a male gender with access to privacy and a watering can, can also improve the nitrogen content!

When it comes to the material content of a compost heap, it should ideally consist equally of a "brown" (dry and dead plant material) and "green" (fresh and often green vegetable waste) content. Rabbit and cavy fanciers will probably find that their cleanings out are the main constituent of the heap and the droppings will help increase the nitrogen content whilst the dead, plant based litter will provide carbon.

Although most weeds can be added to the pile, one must avoid couch grass and bindweed as the former in particular will infest the heap with a multitude of twitch runners. I'm not sure if bindweed would regenerate so leave it out just in case. Unless it can be put to better use (fed to one's stock) compost other weeds and any other waste green material from the garden or kitchen. In this regard, it is surprising how many people think that you cannot compost rhubarb leaves because of the oxalic content. This is not true, as they will rot down and naturalise without any problem; as will beetroot leaves.

Wood ash provides potash, is a rich alkali source and should be spread evenly over the heap. Coal ash cannot be used because of the sulphur content. Coffee grounds are said to be beneficial and can be added as can eggshells that will contribute calcium. Some cardboard can also be added and will provide carbon if more is needed. Human and pet hair is, apparently, high in nitrogen. The dust and fluff from vacuum cleaner bags can also be added to the compost heap.

Grass cuttings are useful but will need to be mixed with other materials to avoid a mushy sludge.

Leaves, I always feel should be kept separate as they rot so slowly and are best put in a black plastic bag when in a damp condition. Tuck them away in a corner and come back in a year's time!

Maturity of the compost heap will vary according to the type of litter used. Wheat straw will break down slower than barley straw and hemp based products are likely to decompose quicker than wood chips. I am probably inclined to use the compost sooner than advisable and rather when I need it. Decomposition is then allowed to continue in the soil over the winter months and I don't seem to experience any problems in this regard.

Composting is hardly an art but rather a case of letting nature take its course and I hope that others will experience the simple satisfaction of getting something very useful out of rubbish, and for so little effort.

Allan Trigg